KINTSUGI

FINDING STRENGTH IN IMPERFECTION

Céline Santini

Andrews McMeel
PUBLISHING®

To my two wonderful ex-husbands,
without whom this book would've never existed.

Kintsugi: Finding Strength in Imperfection

This edition © 2019 by Andrews McMeel Publishing.

Published in French under the title *Kintsugi: L'art de la résilience*
© 2018 by Éditions First, an imprint of Édi8, 12, Avenue d'Italie, 75013 Paris, France

Andrews McMeel Publishing
a division of Andrews McMeel Universal
1130 Walnut Street, Kansas City, Missouri 64106
www.andrewsmcmeel.com

23 24 25 26 27 TEN 10 9 8 7 6 5 4

ISBN: 978-1-4494-9730-9

Library of Congress Control Number: 2018961304

Editor: Mathilde Poncet
Designer: KN Conception
Illustrations: Caroline Donadieu
Photography: Myriam Greff, except for p. 45 Adrien Daste; pp. 189, 190 Céline Santini
Production Editor: Elizabeth A. Garcia
Production Manager: Tamara Haus

ATTENTION: SCHOOLS AND BUSINESSES
Andrews McMeel books are available at quantity discounts with bulk purchase for
educational, business, or sales promotional use. For information, please e-mail the
Andrews McMeel Publishing Special Sales Department: sales@amuniversal.com.

CONTENTS

INTRODUCTION

DISCOVER

蔵焼けて 障るものなき 月見哉

kura yakete / sawaru mono naki / tsukimi kana

————

My storehouse burnt down,
there is nothing to obstruct
the moon view.

Mizuta Masahide
(1657–1723)

EXPLORE

Blessed are the cracked, for they will let the light through.

—Michel Audiard

This book invites you to discover and explore the art of kintsugi in all its facets. This ancestral technique, developed in Japan during the fifteenth century, consists of repairing a broken object by accentuating its cracks with gold—instead of hiding them. But the philosophy behind it goes much deeper than a simple artistic practice. It has to do with the symbolism of healing and resilience. First taken care of and then honored, the broken object accepts its past and paradoxically becomes more robust, more beautiful, and more precious than before it was broken. This metaphor can provide insight into all stages of healing, whether the ailment is physical or emotional.

The word kintsugi comes from the Japanese *kin* (gold) and *tsugi* (joint), literally meaning "golden joint." The art of kintsugi is named *kintsukuroi*, which means "mending with gold." It is a long and extremely detailed process, executed in numerous stages, lasting several weeks—even months. In some cases, it might even take a year to achieve the best kintsugi.

The shards of the broken object are first gathered one by one and then gently cleaned. Then they are glued back together using a traditional lacquer from the Japanese lacquer tree. The object is left to dry, and then it's carefully sanded. Next, the cracks are accentuated with multiple coats of lacquer. Finally, the scars are covered with a metallic powder. Gold powder, or any other powdered metal (silver [*gintsugi* technique], bronze, brass, copper), is dusted on the moist lacquer and melds into it, giving the illusion of streams of flowing metal. After polishing, the object can finally reveal its full brilliance.

Legend has it that the shogun Ashikaga Yoshimasa (1435–1490) always used his favorite tea bowl (*chawan*) for tea ceremony. One day, unfortunately, the bowl broke. Since it had originally come from China, he sent the bowl back there to be repaired. He was, however, extremely disappointed by the result. After waiting many months, the bowl was returned held together with ugly metal clasps that not only disfigured it but also failed to make it watertight. So he asked his Japanese artisans to find a more functional and more aesthetically pleasing solution: The art of kintsugi was born . . .

What an elegant, creative, and simple solution, all in one! Most people who discover the art of kintsugi have an epiphany and fall in love with it at first sight.

The skill is therefore very much in demand. The art of kintsugi is so valued that some connoisseurs have even been known to intentionally break their precious vases or bowls in order to transform them . . . Without going through the trouble of smashing all your valuables, you can be inspired by the kintsugi philosophy through all the different stages of your personal healing process until you rediscover your wholeness and radiance. Like a living kintsugi, you too can be transformed and strengthened by hardship.

Embrace a life of golden beauty.
Discover the spirit of kintsugi.

Wabi-Sabi, Another Idea of Beauty . . .

Kintsugi also fits into the Japanese concept of *wabi-sabi* (*wabi*: humility in the face of natural events; *sabi*: what one feels about the work of time or humanity), inviting you to recognize the beauty of simple, imperfect, and atypical things.

By opening yourself to *wabi-sabi*, you swim against the tide of standardized and artificial modern ideals. *Wabi-sabi* invites contemplation and detachment, rather than perfection. It emphasizes the irreversibility of time and the ephemeral nature of all. It reminds us to appreciate the humble beauty of simple things, patinated by time and the trials of life.

© Myriam Greff

EXPERIMENT

Art helps with living.

—Éric-Emmanuel Schmitt

Kintsugi is the art of exalting past injuries. The Way of Kintsugi can be understood as a kind of art therapy, inviting you to transcend your struggles and transform your personal hardships into gold. It reminds you that your scars, visible or invisible, are proof that you've overcome your difficulties. By marking your history, they demonstrate you've survived, and they enrich your soul.

Even more beautiful,
Even more resilient,
Even more precious,
Even more . . . present!

We all have our own flaws, our own wounds. We've all suffered and lived through difficult times. My own journey, which I'm about to share with you, is filled with joys, pains, accidents, and traumas, as well as bursts of happiness. It's a path like all others, unique in the world and at the same time so universal . . . With its strong symbolism, resolutely based on resilience and optimism, kintsugi has helped me to heal, strengthen myself, and rediscover my breath and my radiance. This is what I want to share with you throughout this book.

No matter what your injury is, physical (car accident, mastectomy, illness, amputation, disability, old age, burns, assault) or emotional (splitting from a friend or lover, divorce, mourning, depression, unemployment, abandonment, rumors, painful childhood), kintsugi's energy can support and accompany you along your healing process. Think of it as an initiatory journey, with your injury as the starting point. As you move through the healing process, you will slowly become stronger and eventually turn into gold, as if by alchemy.

For you, this is the beginning of a new cycle. It's finally your turn to shine . . .

Discover your true self, and uncover a new expression of beauty and perfection. Explore, experiment, execute: This book invites you to get to know this ancestral art and connect with the healing energy of kintsugi.

Heal your wounds.
Transform your fault lines into lines of force,
and turn life's bursts into bursts of laughter.

The Legend of the Broken Vase

As legend has it, a famous tea master of the Japanese emperor, Sen no Rikyū (1522–1591), was once invited to dinner. To honor Rikyū, his host offered him a very old and precious Chinese vase. The tea master wouldn't even look at the gift but instead commented on the beauty of the countryside and admired a tree branch that was gently moving in the wind. After his guest had left, the host shattered the vase in anger and frustration. His friends, a bit wiser than he, collected all the pieces of the broken vase and repaired it using the art of kintsugi. During his next visit, Sen no Rikyū saw the vase with its brilliant golden lines and cried out, "Now it is magnificent!"

© Myriam Greff

10

EXECUTE

*It's the methods we use that
determine the value of a cause.*

—Michel Houellebecq

The art of kintsugi follows a slow and detailed procedure, requiring patience and concentration. Day after day, week after week, step by step, the object is cleaned, reassembled, taken care of, healed, and finally exalted. Here are the detailed steps of the different stages of traditional kintsugi. You might come to like it: It's an opportunity to discover the pleasure of slow and precise actions, an invitation to enthusiastically submerge yourself into total awareness of the present moment.

THE KINTSUGI METHOD:
STEP-BY-STEP REPAIR

STAGE 1: BREAK

Experience: Something unforeseen happens, a wrong move, a shock, and everything falls apart . . .

Accept: Clear your mind and pick up the pieces.

Decide: Make the choice to give the object a second chance, rather than throwing it away.

Choose: Consider the different methods of repair and choose the one that suits you best: the illusionist method (invisible repair), staples (metal clamps along the cracks), or kintsugi (golden joints).

Imagine: Be creative and dare to think differently!

Visualize: Concentrate and imagine the repaired object in all its splendor.

STAGE 2: ASSEMBLE

Prepare: Clean the pieces of the object, gather all the tools (palette knife, palette, lacquer, paintbrush, gold powder, drying box, wooden sticks, turpentine, sandpaper, silk cotton ball), and protect yourself by wearing gloves.

Reconstitute: Examine and assemble the pieces of the "puzzle" to get ready for repair.

Transform: Turn the poison into an antidote! Utilize the natural lacquer (*urushi*) to glue the pieces together. It comes directly from the resin of the lacquer tree, and it's highly toxic, so you must protect yourself while applying it. However, while it dries, it hardens and loses its toxic nature.

Gather: Prepare and apply the glue (*mugi-urushi*, a blend of flour and *urushi* lacquer) to both sides of the fissure with a palette knife, and glue the two pieces together to reconstitute the object.

Fill: If you're missing a piece, prepare a paste (*sabi-urushi*), blending the lacquer (*urushi*) with powdered stone (*tonoko*), and patiently re-create the missing piece with this paste.

Associate: If it inspires you, you can even choose a piece from another object to replace the missing piece (*yobi-tsugi*).

STAGE 3: WAIT

Remove: Scrape off the extra matter with a utensil (razor blade, toothpick, palette knife), and clean using turpentine.

Maintain: Make sure the pieces stay in place by wrapping the object with masking tape or rubber bands.

Breathe: The lacquer (*urushi*) is alive and needs to breathe to dry and to harden. Prepare a covered cardboard box (*muro*), and place a damp towel in the bottom. Using a number of wooden sticks, create a grid so the object can be placed on it.

Pause: The lacquer hardens best at a humidity level of 75 to 90 percent and at a temperature above 68°F. Place the object in this box, maintaining constant temperature and humidity levels.

Clean: Carefully clean your tools (palette knife, palettes, brushes) after each stage with turpentine or vegetable oil, and carefully organize them so they are ready for their next use.

Rest: Patiently leave the object in the box for seven to ten days, until it has dried.

STAGE 4: REPAIR

Polish: Once the object is perfectly dry, clean the excess matter with a scraper and turpentine. Then use sandpaper to completely smooth out the surface. What remain on the object now are nothing but brown scars (*urushi-tsugi*).

Touch: It is sometimes difficult to recognize certain irregularities with the naked eye. Using your fingers and sense of touch, verify that all the joints are perfectly smooth.

Apply: With a small brush, apply a first layer of black lacquer (*roiro-urushi*) to all the joints.

Concentrate: Breathe calmly, concentrate, and execute slowly, using measured and precise gestures to apply thin lines to the joints. Let this first application dry in the box for one to two weeks.

Add: Polish the surface and apply a second fine layer of red lacquer (*e-urushi* or *neri bengara-urushi*).

Reanimate: The joints are finally covered by beautiful red lacquer. Brilliant and free-flowing veins have cured the object to give it a second chance. Put it in the box for half an hour.

STAGE 5: REVEAL

Illuminate: While the lacquer is still moist and sticky, delicately apply the gold powder to the lacquer with a brush or a metal application tool (without touching it, as it is still fresh).

Collect: Save any remaining gold powder for your next creation. Then put the object back into the box for two to three days for drying and hardening.

Emerge: Once the lacquer has dried, use a silk cotton ball to gently remove any excess gold powder.

Protect: To protect the golden joints, apply a fine layer of protective lacquer. After five minutes, gently dab the joints. Then let the object dry for twenty-four hours.

Personalize: Use a tool you like to work with and that appeals to you to polish the golden joints. Some kintsugi masters use agate stones; others use ivory, fish teeth, or hematite stones . . .

Dazzle: To make the gold shine, polish the object with a blend of oil and powder using the polishing tool you have selected.

STAGE 6: SUBLIMATE

Observe: Take a step back and contemplate the repaired and sublimated object in all its uniqueness, strengthened by its veins of gold.

Admire: Notice how the broken object has been reborn and has become a precious work of art, unique and invaluable.

Contemplate: Remember the story behind the scars of the object.

Feel: As the lacquer hardened while drying, feel how the object is even more solid than before.

Welcome: Proudly accept the imperfections of the object. It is even more beautiful and precious once broken and repaired.

Share: Present your creation. Share its history to inspire others that repair is possible.

Kits containing all of the required materials for kintsugi can be easily found on the Internet. Depending upon your perfectionism and your budget, you can follow the traditional method with genuine Japanese lacquer (urushi) and twenty-two-karat gold powder (recommended for alimentary use), or you can simply be inspired by the technique and use epoxy glue and gold paint or nacre powder.

STAGE 1

BREAK

行き行きてたふれ伏とも萩の原

yuki yuki te / tafure fusu tomo / hagi no hara

———————

It doesn't matter where I fall,
as long as it is
in a field of lespedeza.

Kawai Sora
(1649–1710)

**Up until now,
you've survived
100 percent of your
worst experiences.**

EXPERIENCE

During great misfortunes, hearts are broken or strengthened.

—Honoré de Balzac

Something unforeseen happens, a wrong move, a shock, and everything falls apart . . .

You're shattered into a thousand pieces, like a broken object smashed violently on the floor. No matter what awful situation you're experiencing, whether it's physical or psychological, you're under the impression that it can't be overcome. You feel that you'll never get over it or that you'll never be the same person again.

And you're not completely wrong. In fact, *you will never be the same person again.* You will change for the better. This current ordeal is merely an initiation. Consider today the beginning of a long process of reconstruction. Yes, it will be painful. Yes, it will be difficult. Yes, it will take a long time. Why deny it? But it will get better . . .

I have personally experienced this kind of extreme pain, that moment when one feels that everything has fallen apart, several times. When I learned that I was getting divorced, my entire world collapsed in an instant, like a house of cards. I was in shock because I had no clue what might lie ahead for me . . . Marriage represented a special value, a refuge, and I believed it would be a lifelong commitment. In addition, I had experienced my own parents' divorce when I was only four years old. And it was certainly not an accident that I was a wedding planner for the same ten years that my marriage lasted. All of these things made the shock of my divorce particularly difficult, as it made me relive the pain of my childhood, as well as left me alone with a nine-month-old baby. I had no idea how to survive this situation.

However, I am still around today, more resilient and stronger than ever. I did survive. This terrible experience also passed . . . After having worked on healing myself, I did see things far more clearly. I recognized my share of the responsibility. Working on unearthing my winding subconcious, I have identified hidden family patterns. I have rebuilt myself, step-by-step, and have begun to enjoy life again and look forward to the future with confidence. Inspired by this difficult beginning, I never lost hope, and I still find being alive magnificently fulfilling. I regained the courage to get married a second time. Unfortunately, I am now divorced again, but that's another story . . . Someday possibly a third try at marriage? They say that three is the magic number. In spite of my two failed marriages, I still believe in it. After all, according to the famous French saying, "Only by continually trying will one finally succeed. Therefore the more often one fails, the better their chances of succeeding."

Something did fall apart for you today. Events and experiences of your past have injured you deeply. Like an open wound, your flaws and your weaknesses uncover hidden corners of your soul. It is this same place where you will also find unsuspected strength for rebuilding a better version of yourself! Remember: Up until now, you have survived 100 percent of your worst experiences.

The time has come to get ahold of yourself, to take the first steps to be reborn. This step still might be small or hesitant: You're afraid to stumble again . . . Just keep in mind the first step is always the most difficult!

The Legend of the Royal Ring

A Persian legend, whose exact origins have long been lost, tells of a king who asked an old wise man at his court to engrave a golden ring with a quote stating the absolute truth of the world. He desired a sentence that could apply to all situations, for all ages. A quote expressing the meaning of life: words of universal truth.

The old wise man gave the ring back to the king with the following engraving: "This too shall pass."

© Myriam Greff

What About You?

Do you realize how much your previous challenges have contributed to who you are today? Isn't it time to find your joy for life again? Are you looking forward to the pleasant surprises awaiting you in the future?

It's Time to Act!

The Path of Your Life

Take a moment to sit down quietly without interruptions or distractions. This is your time. Create an ideal space to enjoy: soft music, candles, flavored tea, a comfortable chair . . . anything you prefer.

Take a piece of paper and a pen, close your eyes, and relax. Visualize the path of your life, year by year, and remember all the difficult times you have lived through.

Write them down, one by one, while gaining a sense of resilience: You have survived all of these challenges! And deep inside you know that this current situation too will pass!

Go Further . . .

Reflect quietly: Even if you didn't realize it at the time, isn't it true that perhaps some of your most difficult experiences have ironically provided opportunities, like an unexpected gift? Maybe they have allowed you to develop a new sense of self-worth or forced you to learn new skills to escape a bad situation. Or even opened new doors. Thoughtfully contemplate some of your difficult memories, and by doing so, transform your sufferings into strengths. Today, facing these new challenges, you can re-create this personal transformation.

Begin Here and Now!

Why postpone this exercise? Take the first step by picking up a pen and writing down some of your experiences on your list.

Come out of the shadow
into the light . . .

ACCEPT

What's done cannot be undone.

—William Shakespeare

Clear your mind and pick up the pieces.

Like an object that is damaged and broken, your ordeal is upon you. You may still be in shock. Hesitatingly, you pick yourself up, still somewhat dizzy, still a bit groggy.

Everything around you has gone to pieces. What happened?

The time has come to evaluate the situation. It's impossible to go backward. What's done is done . . . This is the moment to accept the inevitable, to welcome what cannot be changed, and to recognize and embrace what is harming you. This phase is necessary to first pull yourself together before you can move forward.

Sometimes the pain may be so intense that the slightest incident revives it all. So your natural reaction may be to ignore it, flee from it, as if denying the problem could make it go away. You may try to protect yourself by quickly hiding away the pieces, removing them to a place as far away as possible. Alternatively you may cover them up completely, smoothing out the surface with a mask of smiles as if everything is okay. And sometimes when you can't stand the pain, you suppress it by all available means, strangling it in any way possible . . .

I know this subject well. My mother had great difficulties accepting her own divorce. Instead of pulling herself together, admitting her share of the responsibility, or asking for help, she was so overcome by grief and depression that alcoholism became the only way to fight her pain. The divorce became a forbidden subject.

It was impossible to talk about it, she did not want to hear it, and she buried her head in the sand like an ostrich . . . As if by denying the existence of the disaster would miraculously make it disappear.

Do not make the same mistake. The hurt still exists in your subconscious! You can certainly pretend that nothing happened, but something certainly did. Something so important that you have no choice but to look it straight in the face rather than to look the other way.

The hurt is a message. In acknowledging it and by embracing it in some form, you can liberate it. This conscious effort is necessary to progress through the steps of healing and, someday, well-being.

It takes courage. It requires you to be honest with yourself, to admit your difficulties rather than to deny or overshadow them.

Even if you can't change the past, you can view it differently. It doesn't have to become something that holds you back but instead can transform you into something better. In order to overcome your suffering, you must first recognize and acknowledge it internally before you can externalize and eventually eliminate it. Come out of the shadow into the light . . .

Kintsugi and Depression

Kintsugi is a beautiful metaphor for the steps of healing depression. In the same way that kintsugi can sublimate a broken object by giving value to its scars, a person suffering from depression can become stronger by accepting his flaws as part of himself.

This suffering is the beginning of something else. It can help you understand yourself more deeply and overcome your ordeals. With the help of therapy, you will discover your true self.

And with your suffering and depression behind you, you will become a new person, undoubtedly more sensitive and probably much stronger. Your scars bear witness. Suffering and depression are from now on an integral part of your history. Kintsugi teaches you to be proud of them and to hold your head high. Accept this painful past that makes you unique.

What About You?

Are you always honest with yourself? Do you know how to recognize your sufferings and to listen to them, or do you sometimes have a tendency to stifle them and censor yourself?

It's Time to Act!

The Message from Your Body

Find a quiet time in order to practice the following exercise:

To begin, take several deep breaths and relax completely. Close your eyes. When completely calm, connect with your body and feel its sensations. Think about the misfortune you are actually living through and about what exactly makes you suffer: What do you feel? How does this express itself in your body? Maybe tears fill your eyes? Or you feel a heavy weight on your chest? Shortness of breath? Your heart races fast and hard? Fear sits like a pit in your stomach? Or all of these things at the same time? These are only examples. Concentrate on your own body's sensations.

Once you have identified these feelings, choose one of them. This pain conveys an emotion. It's there to signal the presence of a problem, and it will continue to be there until the problem has gone away. That is its mission.

Don't look away: Accept the problem's existence. Get in touch with the part of you that makes you suffer, and let yourself feel it in all of its intensity. Identify the type of emotion you are suffering from. Without trying to avoid the pain, look at it calmly, as if through a magnifying glass, and try to progressively relax about it. Feel grateful for this sensation and be thankful for its action. It has done its work as a witness. If you really concentrate calmly and with gentleness, the suffering will disappear.

If you feel other uncomfortable body sensations, simply repeat this exercise.

Open your eyes and let your entire being absorb the disappearance of the painful sensation. Your overall tension has probably diminished as well. If this exercise has made you feel better, you should regularly repeat it as soon as you feel an unpleasant body sensation.

Go Further . . .

Express the full power of your emotions through intense activities that make you burst out shouting or laughing! For example, boxing, a tribal dance, a primal scream, a tickling session, theater performances, a pillow fight, and so on . . . whatever works for you.

Start Here and Now!

Close your eyes, breathe deeply, and begin to concentrate on your innermost self. Let these thoughts flow . . .

Honor yourself!

DECIDE

The true perfection of man lies, not in what man has, but in what man is.

—Oscar Wilde

Make the choice to give the object a second chance, rather than throwing it away.

Convince yourself that you can be like the broken object repaired by the kintsugi technique. You are a valuable jewel that deserves to be healed with gold, one of the most precious metals on the planet. You are invaluable and are worth the best. In deciding to repair what has been broken, you not only simply recognize its value but add sentiment to the object. As in the art of kintsugi, in deciding to take control of your life in spite of the sufferings experienced, you give yourself an invaluable gift: your self-esteem!

After my second divorce (only one year after being married), I really hit rock bottom. I had a second baby to raise by myself, and my family's divorce history was repeating itself as if predetermined. My pattern of failures, one after the other, including a career without a clear path, made me feel like I was wasting my life and hadn't accomplished anything. Do you also sometimes feel that you lack any redeeming value?

A friend helped me pick myself up by pointing out my accomplishments. I had raised two daughters with much goodwill and love. I had found the courage to change my life several times, including the two businesses I had started. I had tried many different professions, including wedding planner, project manager for a design agency, fragrance development manager for the flavor and fragrance industry, wedding celebrant, product manager at L'Oréal, personal-development and art therapy coach, brainstorming leader, marketing and promotion professor, and author. I had created all of these with my own willpower. I had found a way to overcome the impossible and to create my own reality each time I really wanted something. I had even found resilience after my mother's suicide. My friend reminded me that my life was meaningful and that I had accomplished much more than I realized.

No matter what your path and accomplishments might be, never forget your own precious value. Just as an object can be restored with gold and many hours of painstaking effort, you too deserve the same attention, the same time, and the same investment. Consciously decide to take care of yourself, but also let others take care of you too. If you settle for masking or covering your wounds, they might open again. Make the decision to really recover. Patiently add layer after layer to help yourself heal over time. You deserve it! Honor yourself!

The Film *It's a Wonderful Life*

Along these lines, I highly recommend you see Frank Capra's masterpiece *It's a Wonderful Life* (1946). This film with old-fashioned charm portrays a desperate man ready to take his own senseless life when an angel appears to him. The angel points out how important his life on Earth has been and how much his natural goodness has influenced the lives of many others. To his own amazement, he realizes his true value and the merits of his existence.

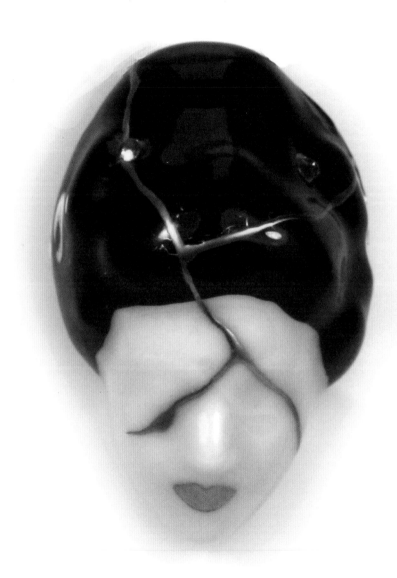

What About You?

Do you know your own worth, or do you have a tendency to underestimate yourself? And if you were to list your merits right now, what would they be?

It's Time to Act!

The List of Your Accomplishments

You too should start to appreciate your worth and your value as a precious jewel! On a piece of paper or a digital screen, list your accomplishments. Include the major ones, but don't forget the minor successes too. Everything you do well in your life matters. Think about your strengths and those activities you succeed at naturally. Include the things that come easily to you for which you are often complimented. Accept your success without false modesty. These writings are only for you to read.

Low self-esteem can make this a difficult exercise. Sadly, we don't usually honor ourselves (what a shame!). If this sounds like you, start by complimenting yourself on your small, daily successes: I baked a delicious lemon tart, or I know how to change a tire. Progressively move to more important qualities such as, I am a good father, I am patient, and people like to confide in me. And finally some real successes in your life: I have raised two marvelous children, I doubled the financial results of my company, I restored an old barn with my own two hands, and so on.

A small but important side note: We often have the tendency to underestimate our merits, not because of modesty but ignorance. We tend to consider the things that we accomplish easily as normal or banal. We value these simple accomplishments less. Since I'm able to write with ease, I have the tendency to not list this skill. I forget that not everyone can write as easily as I do. On the other hand, I am absolutely useless when it comes to directing a team. I admire this competence of a friend who doesn't even acknowledge his special talent. He thinks it's normal to have this skill.

Simply list all your skills without any edits, rankings, or value judgments.

_____

_____

_____

_____

_____

_____

_____

_____

_____

_____

_____

_____

_____

_____

_____

_____

Admire all of your successes . . . You really are a valuable person!

Go Further . . .

Ask your friends and family to help you complete this list. Expect a few surprises.

Begin Here and Now!

Fill in the first line to get started.

Follow your innermost
momentum!

CHOOSE

You must choose among the dreams that warm your soul the most.

—Louis-Ferdinand Céline

Consider the different methods of repair and choose the one that suits you best: the illusionist method (invisible repair), staples (metal clamps along the cracks), or kintsugi (golden joints).

Just like when fixing a broken object, you have to find your own viable method in order to heal yourself. Do you prefer to cover up your hurts quickly? Do you use a smooth yet careful manner to cover your facade, giving the impression that all is well (illusionary technique)? What about a fast but very visible cure (stapled technique)? Or do you prefer to take your time to really heal your scars, so that your wounds do not open again, by taking pride in the scars that make you unique (art of kintsugi)?

Each technique has its own advantages and disadvantages. There is no good or bad answer. All depends on your available time, your motivation, and your path in life. There comes a time in life when it is difficult to repair and analyze oneself all alone, mainly because there are too many self-help techniques to choose from. Therefore, do not hesitate to seek help from a therapist, a book, a seminar, a course, or an Internet conference.

Over the years, I have personally explored many different options, some emotional, others more physical: hypnosis, writing, meditation, mindfulness-based stress reduction (MBSR), theater, spiral dynamics, yoga, clown workshop, energetic method, fasciatherapy, acupuncture, mandala, clay block therapy, logotherapy, family constellations, Chinese medicine, chi gong, *chi nei tsang*, overtone singing, inner child, Pilates, laughter yoga, theater improv, feng shui, psychogenealogy, chiropractics, geobiology, Emotional Freedom Technique (EFT), osteopathy, and, above all, kintsugi!

Sometimes one finds the perfect therapy instantly. But more often exploring several different paths is necessary until multiple methods produce a group of complementary answers. I call this the cocktail effect of personal development. Each action is in itself effective, but when combined, their impact is amplified. What resonates with you? Follow your innermost momentum!

THE DIFFERENT REPAIR TECHNIQUES
Illusionary Repair

The repair is invisible. The scars certainly exist, but they are perfectly masked. If done well, the object appears to be new, its past well hidden.

Repairing with Metal Clasps (Staples)

The repair is quite visible with the different pieces being held together by metallic clasps. This was the initial method used for the Shogun's tea bowl, but he was so disappointed with the results that he asked his artisans to invent a different method, and kintsugi was born.

The Art of Kintsugi

The repair is not only visible but emphasized by highlighting it with gold. The object's past is taken into consideration, thus transforming it into a unique, precious, and irreplaceable object.

What About You?

Are you ready to try a new personal-development technique and ask for some support in your healing process? Could you let your enthusiasm carry you forward?

It's Time to Act!

The Different Personal-Development Techniques

Relax, rid yourself of all thoughts, and read the list below. Listen to your intuition to discover whether any of the techniques that follow immediately speak to you. This list is simply a starting point for inspiration, without any preferences. Certainly, some of these overlap, when the body is caring for the mind and vice versa. These groups are only my suggestions, and it's not possible to give you all the details here. Glean from the list below and use what inspires you.

Physical paths: yoga, running, obstacle course racing, climbing, Pilates, martial arts, boxing, healthy nutrition, vegetarianism, fasting, osteopathy, fasciatherapy, acupuncture, reflexology, naturopathy, Chinese medicine, balneotherapy, *chi nei tsang*, shiatsu, hydrotherapy, chiropractics, etc.

Emotional paths: psychotherapy, psychoanalysis, spiral dynamics, laughter yoga, hypnosis, mindfulness meditation, improv, MBSR, eye movement desensitization and reprocessing (EMDR), EFT, clown workshop, nonviolent communication, rebirth, Gestalt therapy, positive psychology, primal therapy, logotherapy, Alexander, etc.

Sensitivity paths: Bach flowers, kinesiology, hippotherapy, massages, aromatherapy, dancing, music therapy, overtone singing, Tibetan bowls, chromotherapy, Feldenkrais method, tantrism, etc.

Energy paths: energy harmonization care, feng shui, geobiology, chi gong, tai chi, Reiki, shamanism, magnetism, lithotherapy, etc.

Systemic or family paths: psychogenealogy, family constellations, inner child, etc.

Artistic paths: mandala, clay block therapy, writing, calligraphy, theater, art therapy, painting, drawing, sculpture, pottery, kintsugi, etc.

Go Further . . .

Buy a book about your chosen subject, or learn more about your favorite method by checking out the Internet, videoconferences, and interviews.

Start Here and Now!

Circle all the techniques that appeal to you, even if you don't know why . . .

**To change your life,
something in your life
has to change . . .**

IMAGINE

No problem can be solved from the same level of consciousness that created it.

—Albert Einstein

Be creative and dare to think differently!

When we break an object, our first reaction might be to throw it away, or to repair it superficially, so that the break isn't visible.

The art of kintsugi, however, proposes to approach the problem from the opposite intent. Instead of hiding the fissures, kintsugi suggests to emphasize them and even embellish them. Instead of losing its value, the object becomes even more precious than before it was broken. This is the message in Edgar Allan Poe's famous short story *The Purloined Letter*, where a stolen letter is displayed instead of being hidden. Creative thinking is often described as thinking outside of the box. The French equivalent translates literally into "leaving the trodden path." Look for solutions outside your normal routines. Albert Einstein was fond of remarking that the definition of madness is expecting different results when doing the same thing over and over again. It would therefore appear reasonable to look for solutions by going in a different direction and thinking differently.

At the beginning of my career, I often changed my job but never felt fulfilled, to the point where every morning I felt sick about having to go back to work. Finally, one day I realized that all my problems came from not being well suited to work in a corporate environment. If I wanted to stop being unhappy at work, I needed to look at things differently. I realized that in my heart I had always truly wanted to be self-employed and create my own business. Three days after this epiphany, I began the adventure of starting my own wedding planning business. That was 2003 when this kind of business did not yet exist in France! I had to change my routine and try something different. I had to think outside the box.

If you always do the same thing, you risk limiting yourself to the same results forever. In order to break the cycle of the same methods, it's necessary to envision things from a different perspective. To change your life, something in your life has to change . . .

The Spirit of Kintsugi

The spirit of kintsugi can even translate to interior design. Each fissure, each crack can become beautiful and provide an opportunity to breathe new life into an object or a building. An excellent example of this is the Parisian restaurant Anahi. In order to preserve the original hundred-year-old integrity of this location, the owners carefully repaired it by filling and highlighting the old cracks with copper leaf.

© Adrien Daste

What About You?

Do you have a tendency to use the same methods over and over and then complain about the same unsatisfactory results? What would happen if you started thinking differently and changed just one aspect of your life?

It's Time to Act!

The Power of Brainstorming

During one of my previous lives, while working in the marketing department for a flavor and fragrance company, I was in charge of facilitating brainstorming sessions. During these meetings we produced many ideas, but they were not necessarily always related to each other. None of these ideas were given any priority, at least at the beginning of the process. It was only during a second session that we began to attach value to them. Try using one of these techniques to inspire your own creativity. The SCAMPER technique, whose name is derived from the first letters of the suggested actions, is an invitation to see things differently.

In thinking about what gets in your way, try to . . .

S : Substitute

C : Combine

A : Adapt

M : Modify

P : Put to another use

E : Eliminate

R : Reverse

Go Further . . .

Another efficient creativity technique is mind mapping, also called mental mapping or heuristic scheme. It uses a diagram to help classify and clarify your ideas, thus leading to the creation of new ones. Write down a problem or a topic in the center of a page. Draw a circle around it. All other ideas emerge from this central statement. From there you create idea branches related to the central statement, intuitively classifying your thoughts. This very visual technique can incorporate significant symbols for you, like different colors for different categories. You can thus immediately see what is missing, associate different ideas, complement them, and refine them by adding supplementary branches, etc.

I have used the heuristic technique all my life to organize my ideas. It was useful to prepare essay plans, to find new ideas when I worked in marketing, to prepare proposals for my wedding planning, and also to find new book ideas. I have been using it for each question in my life whenever I've had to make a decision. I have a whole notebook covering the last twenty years, and it gives me great pleasure to immerse myself in it from time to time.

If this method inspires you, I invite you to use this tool to help you find and classify your ideas, to internalize them, and most importantly, to clarify them!

Start Here and Now!

Take a piece of paper and write down your most important problem in the center. Draw a circle around it. This is the beginning of your brainstorming session and the center of your first mental map.

Visualize a better
version of yourself!

VISUALIZE

Vision is the art of seeing things invisible.

—Jonathan Swift

Concentrate and imagine the repaired object in all its splendor.

Before starting to work on the broken object, the kintsugi master first imagines what it will look like when it's splendidly restored. This is a good metaphor for your own life. It is, after all, well known that the brain can program itself to act in both a positive or negative mode. What are the repetitive actions of your own programming? What kind of thoughts are you feeding your brain with? Do you have a long-term vision? And could you reprogram yourself?

I had already recognized the power of visualization as a teenager. I went through perplexing and complex times. I went from a smiling, sweet, four-year-old girl with a sunny disposition to an ugly duckling when my parents divorced. I isolated myself from the rest of the world and became an abnormally shy, troubled introvert. I have to admit that my thick glasses, braces, and chubby little stomach didn't help either. I preferred to stay hidden, out of the spotlight.

However, when I was fifteen, I read about the power of visualization in a teen magazine. I suddenly realized that I could and wanted to change things. I visualized a better version of myself each and every day.

I covered all the walls in my room with stimulating and inspiring images, like a huge visualization board. In addition, theater tryouts helped to improve my self-esteem.

Visualization nourished me and allowed me to hatch and to come out of my shell. Today I accept my strengths, my weaknesses, and my eccentricities, and I have no problem speaking in public. I accept who I am.

So you too can project your future successes and accomplishments onto an internal imaginary screen. Visualize a better version of yourself!

The Power of Visualization

Many scientific studies have attested to the power of visualization.

One can use it to treat unreasonable fear, to anticipate stressful situations, to prepare oneself for a medical procedure, to improve one's memory, or to aid the healing process . . .

For example, visualization is a well-known sports training technique. Athletes can significantly improve their performance by visualizing well-executed movements and success before a sports event.

There are two basic kinds of visualization. Realistic visualization is based on real situations, such as using all five senses to visualize speaking in public for instance. Symbolic visualization uses metaphors, such as imagining a problem in the shape of a black cloud, protecting oneself with a bubble of light. It's up to you to find the best technique that suits you.

For all situations it is thus possible to imagine a visualization of success. It seems that the brain uses the same circuits for real and imaginary situations and, therefore, does not differentiate between the two. So you might as well nourish your brain with beautiful thoughts.

What About You?

What is particularly important to you? What if you start today by visualizing your successes and your wounds already healed?

It's Time to Act!

The Vision Board

A vision board can be a powerful tool to address your subconscious at the time when you create it and on a daily basis after. It is a method that works by positioning images that inspire and stimulate you side by side.

Define the format from the beginning. It is best to choose a large format (for example, twenty by thirty inches). You can attach the elements to a piece of cardboard, a frame, a large sheet of paper, or even on a magnetic board, to update regularly.

❶ Gather a variety of magazines. Ideally, these should contain many general images with subjects that attract you spontaneously. (This is also the time to ask yourself what captivates your attention the most.)

❷ Instinctively and without overthinking, scan each magazine and cut out the pages that interest you. Proceed in the spirit of brainstorming without any restrictions or hesitation.

❸ Cut out the separate images and place them side by side on your board. Search, reattach, replace, and rearrange until you like the result.

❹ Sit back and look at your creation. Certain choices will surprise you. This is your subconscious speaking to you through these images.

❺ Your board can be kept secret or shared with some close friends so they can help you interpret your creation.

❻ Look at your creation every day and concentrate: What you see there represents a condensed version of your aspirations. Little by little, the images will become a part of you, to inspire your new adventure.

Go Further . . .

Mental movies is another efficient visualization technique. Project positive images by visualizing successful situations onto your internal, imaginary screen. If you do this regularly, your brain will progressively register the new information.

Start Here and Now!

Pick up the first magazine that's close by and cut out the first image!

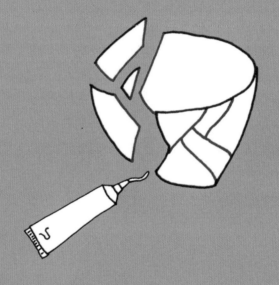

STAGE 2

ASSEMBLE

砕けても砕けてもあり水の月

Kudakete mo / kudakete mo / ari mizu no tsuki

———————

The moon in the water;
broken and broken again,
still it is there.

—Ueda Chōshū
(1852–1932)

**Here and now,
enjoy the presents
of the present.**

PREPARE

In the fields of observation chance favors only the prepared mind.

—Louis Pasteur

Clean the pieces of the object, gather all the tools (palette knife, palette, lacquer, paintbrush, gold powder, drying box, wooden sticks, turpentine, sandpaper, silk cotton balls), and protect yourself by wearing gloves.

While preparing for his work, the kintsugi master is not in a hurry. First, he steps back, evaluates, prepares, and carefully arranges his materials. He takes his time with slow, precise, and measured gestures. He knows that once the procedure starts, time is of the essence and he cannot afford to make any mistakes. This is why it's essential that everything is organized and accessible before the actual work begins, like a surgical operation. This step may appear to be unnecessary, but this ritual of preparation is already part of the healing process.

Just as the materials for kintsugi are carefully assembled, you can prepare yourself with care before starting your own healing process. Take a step back, slow down, and get ready for the sacred event of your own transformation.

This method was new to me at first. All my life I had the tendency to rush ahead at one hundred miles per hour. My motto? Fast and efficient. I was focused on managing my business, blind to our problems as a couple, and always in a hurry and under stress. I didn't realize I was heading straight into a wall. At times, life has its own sense of humor:

Instead of letting me move straight ahead with force, it derailed me straight into a ditch, literally. On a day like any other, while racing to go home, I missed a curve in the road, resulting in a serious automobile accident. The car was reduced to twisted metal. By some miracle, I only suffered a very small wound above my left eye. My first gash, whose scar I cherish still today. It was like a wake-up call, trying to alert me. But I didn't get the message, and I continued faster and faster straight for the wall that was looming ahead. Until one day my life blew up, when I got divorced. And then, one year after, when my mother committed suicide. This time I had no choice but to stop.

These life-changing events took me a long time to address. However, now I realize that they led me to the path of mindfulness. At first I suffered enormously, totally removed from my comfort zone. I sat immobilized on my meditation pillow, suffering through the thousands of pains in my neck and what felt like ants devouring my feet, but most of all the overwhelming impatience!

Today I greatly enjoy the ritual of meditation. But it is mostly during my day-to-day activities that I am really conscious of my progress. My movements have slowed down, and I approach with deliberation and pleasure even the most ordinary tasks, savoring each instant.

Life is quirky; ironically, circumstances forced me to drive again. For me, a two-hour daily commute is anything but fun. Lately, rather than complaining about the traffic jams, I have learned to appreciate the "here and now." I see these intervals that would have been insignificant or even disagreeable in the past in a positive new light and the beginning of being fully conscious. I still have a long way to go, but I understand that I have all the time to get there.

"When you eat, eat; when you walk, walk." I love this Zen concept. I have made it my new mantra. How many times have you eaten a piece of cake without really tasting it? The piece might already be gone before you even noticed it was there! Or drank a quick cup of coffee? The cup might already be empty before you tasted anything . . . "Here and now" is really the only moment that counts, because the past doesn't exist anymore and the future isn't here yet. Life is nothing but a sequence of small, fleeting moments. If you are consciously aware of this fact, you too will be able to take a measured step back with pleasure instead of rushing ahead. With your head held high, feel and enjoy each moment as if it were the most important of your life: It actually is! Here and now, enjoy the presents of the present.

The Zen Monk and the Umbrella

Legend has it that one day a Zen monk went to see his master. After many years of practice, he felt ready to become a master himself.

It was a rainy day, and as traditional custom, he left his shoes and his umbrella at the door.

Once standing before his master, he offered his respects and said, "Master, I have been following your teachings for years. Am I ready?"

The master looked at him with gentleness and said to him, "To begin with, please tell me one thing. When you arrived, you took off your shoes and left your umbrella. Did you put your umbrella on the right side or left side of your shoes?"

The disciple was surprised. He had not anticipated such a question, and answered, "I haven't the slightest idea!"

The master responded to him, "So you are not ready yet. How was the moment, when you placed down your umbrella, less important than any other? You will be ready when you pay attention to each and every moment of your life, no matter what."

What About You?

Are you consciously aware that each moment is precious, or do you rush at times without savoring life? Are you ready to become mindfully present for every instant of your life?

It's Time to Act!

Mindfulness Meditation

Have you ever tried mindfulness meditation? It's based on a fairly "easy" principle. It consists of focusing your mind on the present moment and observing your thoughts and sensations. There is no right or wrong way to achieve this. It could be a long path, day after day, for you to discover your own rhythm. However, the many benefits of stress reduction, a better outlook on life, and letting go may be realized surprisingly fast. If you practice regularly, you will gradually feel encouraged by your initial results, because very quickly the neuronal "circuits of awareness" are strengthened. You will progressively become more conscious of the present, be better focused, and feel more alive.

If this subject interests you, there are many options to explore. Personally, I followed mindfulness-based stress reduction (MBSR) training. The two-month program developed by Jon Kabat-Zinn, who has revived the interest in mindfulness, is a good place to begin. You can also consult numerous books, the Internet, conferences, workshops, etc.

Here is a brief introduction for you to discover mindfulness meditation:

- Set an alarm for a duration of your choice. You can begin with one minute, increasing it by one minute every day. Once you get comfortable, increase the intervals to five or ten minutes. (In order to emerge gently, use a friendly alarm sound, such as a gong or wind chime, not a buzzer.) Initially it does not seem like very long, but before you know it, you'll work your way up to thirty minutes.

- Sit down comfortably, with your back straight, on a meditation pillow or a chair. Do not lie down to avoid falling asleep.

- Start by paying attention to your breath.

- Observe your body sensation without making any judgments.

- Each time an idea comes into your head, contemplate it, and then let it flow away.

- That's all. It is as "simple" as that.

Go Further . . .

Mindfulness can be practiced formally through meditation but also by observing small gestures of daily life, such as washing dishes, cleaning your house, watching your children, kneading bread dough, or savoring a meal. In fact, it's as "simple" as being 100 percent mindful of all of your actions.

Start Here and Now!

Set your alarm for one minute. Sit up straight and try!

Assemble, count, and number
the jigsaw puzzle pieces
of your life.

RECONSTITUTE

Until you are broken you don't know what you're made of.

—Ziad K. Abdelnour

Examine and assemble the pieces of the "puzzle" to get ready for repair.

The kintsugi master also takes time to assemble the "puzzle" of the objects he intends to take care of. He juxtaposes each piece, takes note of the cracks and missing pieces, evaluates and anticipates the difficulties of reconstruction, numbers the pieces, and finally decides the order in which he will proceed.

In life as in the art of kintsugi, it is sometimes necessary to take the time for evaluating a situation, to ask oneself pertinent questions, and to reconstitute the "puzzle" of your journey. This phase requires taking a step back in order to get to know yourself better. In first identifying the repetitive actions of your life, the recurring problems, the beliefs that inspire you to act, your patterns, you can eliminate obstructions and move forward. Nonetheless, it is always easier to see others' weaknesses before clearly seeing our own. Ironically, as much as we may easily identify others' patterns, it may be difficult for us to observe our own! Without realizing it, we commonly repeat the same patterns and subconsciously make the same mistakes. So how then do we proceed without being a prisoner of our repeated actions?

For a long time I was oblivious to my own repetitive behaviors. A friend pointed out to me that she found it "interesting" that, despite my fear, I had repeated my parents' behavior by divorcing, twice! By trying to avoid this pattern at all costs,

I had actually reproduced it. It took me a long time to understand that I was dealing with a symptom rather than the initial wound. This touched on something deeply rooted within myself, the emotional damage that, as far back as I can remember, led me to make bad emotional choices out of a need for security. It was only by finally recognizing the initial emotional damage that I was able to finally move on, hoping to break the pattern this time!

Examining your early life can shed light on your present situation. What kind of behavior are you likely to repeat, without knowing why? As if this force was stronger than your own self? Could it be that it reminds you of some pain caused by part of your family's past?

It is your turn to assemble, count, and number the "jigsaw" pieces of your life. Finally, when you have it all together, you will start to see the patterns of your life.

© Myriam Greff

Jigsaw Therapy

When was the last time you did a jigsaw puzzle? Maybe when you were a child? Yet, putting a jigsaw puzzle together has all kinds of unexpected benefits:

- Improving concentration
- Feeling fully conscious and alert
- Developing endurance
- Learning to be patient
- Developing a sense of order
- Clearing the mind
- Developing a sense for strategy and reflexes
- Feeling a sense of accomplishment
- Getting in touch with your inner child

In working a puzzle, you automatically lose all sense of time and are immersed in a bubble of concentration. By handling the pieces, you subconsciously organize your thoughts, and you also get to experience the joy of laying down the last piece . . .

What About You?

Have you identified the recurring patterns in your life, the familiar beliefs that manipulate you and prevent you from moving forward? Are you ready to change the theme of your puzzle?

It's Time to Act!

The Jigsaw Puzzle of Your Life

In order to take a good look at your life, I invite you to create a puzzle of your journey:

❶ Prepare a blank jigsaw puzzle with a piece of cardboard, or use the back of an existing puzzle, or even buy one (you can find online some blank puzzles in any shape, even in the shape of a heart, if that inspires you).

❷ On a white piece of paper, without thinking too much, write down all the words you can think of that represent all the recurring themes of your life (whether good or bad). Include anything that spontaneously seems important to you, even if you don't know why. Here are a few examples: children, entrepreneurship, perfume, travels, divorce, pedagogy, writing, beauty, light, vocation, transmission, books, love, kintsugi, multitasking, creativity, accident, and resilience.

For example, think about your accomplishments, your successes and your failures, your key moments, your passions, words that inspire you, symbols that speak to you . . . everything that regularly comes back into your life, like a chorus of a song.

❸ This list will be surprising and eclectic, but it looks like you.

❹ Fine-tune it and clean it up, until it perfectly represents your life.

❺ Now copy the words onto the pieces of the blank puzzle you prepared.

❻ Sit back and study the puzzle of your life!

❼ What strikes you? What are the recurring themes? Which words do you like best? And which the least? Which pieces would you like to change or eliminate?

Go Further . . .

Contemplate your jigsaw puzzle a little more and then redo it. This time, select the pieces you want to keep, the ones that make you happy, and discard the others. Start over with a newly prepared puzzle, just like the first one. Put it back together only with the happy words that please you and fill the empty spaces with new key words that correspond with your aspirations. Eliminate the patterns you would like to get rid of.

Start Here and Now!

Now choose the jigsaw puzzle to get started!

Transform your poison
into an antidote!

TRANSFORM

Nothing is lost, nothing is created, everything is transformed.

—Antoine-Laurent de Lavoisier

Turn the poison into an antidote! Utilize the natural lacquer (*urushi*) to glue the pieces together. It comes directly from the resin of the lacquer tree, and it's highly toxic, so you must protect yourself while applying it. However, while it dries, it hardens and loses its toxic nature.

Get inspired by the kintsugi process to face your inner demons and transform them. Often the solution is right before your eyes. Changing a small detail can sometimes be sufficient. For example, for a long time I was a prisoner of an addiction. The definition of an addiction is when you start to ritualize an impulse and that same stimulus (every Friday, each time I party, every day when I come home, etc.) triggers an irrepressible desire. You crave it. The idea of doing without it starts to make you uncomfortable. You're perfectly aware that it's a bad idea . . . but it's more powerful than you. And afterward you feel so bad, even nauseated, for having done the same mistake again.

For me this was an addiction to eating chips with dried sausage (before I became a vegetarian!). Every Tuesday evening, this ritual forced me to get my fix. Why this particular day? Simply because on Tuesday evenings, I didn't have custody of my daughter. Significantly, these kinds of addictions often manifest themselves on those days when you let off steam, so usually on the weekend.

At first, it might seem kind of funny, and this addiction might not appear to be so bad, but after several months . . . I was starting to feel like an alcoholic needing his fix. One day while I was in line at the supermarket, I suddenly remembered my hidden, inner little girl who had observed my mother stashing her weekly three bottles of whiskey at the bottom of her shopping basket.

That was the day I decided to do something. But how could I break my well-entrenched, ritualized habit that was ready to reappear as an uncontrollable desire? What would prevent me from falling back on this same habit a week later? By simply adapting the ritual (at least to start with), and changing one important key factor, I fooled my subconscious. The trigger for me was "Tuesday night." I decided not to fight it, as the reflex was too well embedded, but instead decided to replace my usual fix. I chose to eat something really healthy instead. For me, that was sushi. By replacing a guilty pleasure with a healthy one, you don't feel distraught. The subconscious is pleasantly surprised and concentrates on other things, which slowly permits you to abandon the entire ritual, because after a few months, it doesn't have any reason to exist anymore. It's a bit like distracting a child with a new toy.

What is your poison? The habit that you would like to change? Rather than trying to be completely immune to the ritual, first try transforming the bad habit gradually, little by little. Change your guilty pleasures into healthy ones: Transform your poison into an antidote!

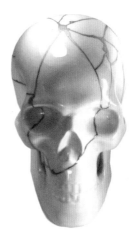

© Myriam Greff

Kintsugi and Alchemy

Kintsugi and alchemy have much in common . . .

As the alchemist tries to transform lead into gold, the kintsugi master adds gold to transmute the imperfections into something precious, attempting to prolong the life of an object entrusted to his care, as if using an elixir of long life. He will use a slow and ritualized process, applying successive layers of lacquer in black and red, reminiscent of the blackening and reddening stages of the alchemy process. As an alchemist, he will work the four elements (air that circulates in the *muro*, earth with powder of *tonoko*, water added to *sabi*, and the fire of gold) to combine them using heat and humidity. (In alchemy, "heat activated in a humid environment results in blackening," which is a reminder of a kintsugi drying within the shelter of his *muro*.)

The ground and pulverized First Matter (materia prima) is separated, just as the broken parts of the kintsugi are. Both methods are used to purify and associate opposite matters into a combination of a new and more splendid existence, transmuting the First Matter toward a new consciousness.

In that, kintsugi is a true alchemistic process.

What About You?

What are your own "poisons"? Do you have well-embedded, toxic habits? Are they always triggered by the same circumstances? Which detail could you alter to get more positive results?

It's Time to Act!

The Alchemistic Transformation of Your Poison

Start by identifying your own poisons. Do you engage in a pleasant little ritual on a daily or even weekly basis? Maybe it's not really a problem: After all, "the dose makes the poison." (Paracelsus)

But if it's something:

❶ Bad for you

❷ And you have trouble getting rid of it

The time has probably come to do something about it . . .

List the bad habits ("guilty pleasures") you would like to change, and try to identify what triggers them.

Guilty Pleasure	Triggering Mechanism	Healthy Pleasure

For each guilty pleasure, write down a detail that can be changed. You are trying to replace this bad habit with a new object or activity that you find more pleasing and motivating, the "healthy pleasure."

For example, if the habit you want to change is "smoking too much" (the guilty pleasure), and your trigger is "I always start smoking Friday evening when I party with my friends" (triggering mechanism), then pick one detail to change and write it under the "healthy pleasure" column: "Go to a hammam on Friday nights instead."

Go Further ...

At least during the first few weeks, have a close friend meet you, so he/she can support you when that trigger moment hits you.

Start Here and Now!

In your weekly agenda, note right now the solution for the first change of habit.

Reconnect with your
inner promise . . .

GATHER

*The soul is a lyre on which all
the strings should be played.*

—George Sand

Prepare and apply the glue (*mugi-urushi*, a blend of flour and *urushi* lacquer) to both sides of the fissure with a palette knife, and glue the two pieces together to reconstitute the object.

This phase is crucial. After a long and careful preparation, the kintsugi master finally has all the pieces on hand to reconstitute the object. He is now ready to begin an effective cure to give the object its original oneness.

For you too, the time has come to begin a patient reassembling of the pieces of your soul. It's time to reconnect to your true self. But do you even know who you really are? Do you feel complete and one? True to yourself? True to your soul? True to your initial promise?

At times, while well on your way, it's easy to lose sight of yourself. In the midst of your turbulent life, you forget childhood promises and key resolutions. Instead you engage in dull, empty, soulless experiments. Deep inside, something is lacking . . . But what?

For a long time I had these same sensations. I felt like an empty shell that had left pieces of myself elsewhere. All my personal-development goals were, therefore, focused on recognizing my soul, my creativity, and my mission in life.

For me, it took three different creative arts to reconnect: dance, music, and writing. These were everything that had given me joy as a child, but they had practically disappeared from my life. If you had asked me just five years ago, I would have told you that I didn't like music at all and only had a minor interest in dance and writing. That belief was blocking my energy so strongly that it couldn't circulate at all. A year after reconnecting with these three arts, I felt truly enlightened! It was as if a door suddenly opened and fresh air entered my life. I was finally back in my element after rediscovering myself. At last, I could breathe deeply and finally reconnect with myself.

All the signs had been there since my childhood. I loved dancing, walked around everywhere with my portable record player, and devoured books, reading anything I could get my hands on. I would regularly hide under the covers at night to finish a book! When asked what I wanted to be later in life, I answered, "A writer!" I had buried these desires deep within my soul for many years. They sometimes showed up fleetingly: an evening out with friends to go dancing, the journals I kept writing, my inner child who invited me to dance when I met with her through meditation, etc. But then I buried them again, even deeper. When all of this finally became unblocked, the pieces of the jigsaw puzzle could be reassembled. I had finally found a part of myself and reconnected with my soul.

Often, the indications exist for a long time, perhaps forever, right under your nose. You just forgot to follow them! But it is never too late to collect the small, scattered pieces of your soul and to put them together.

To reassemble oneself is to rediscover what always really moved and excited you. It might have been in the shadows of your life for years. Now it is time to get realigned and newly unified. Reconnect with your inner promise . . .

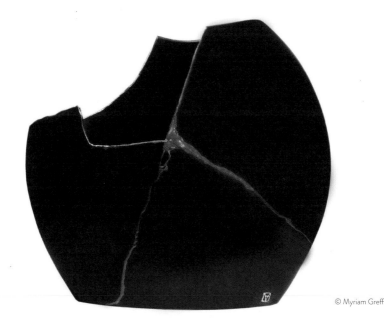

© Myriam Greff

What About You?

Do you feel complete and one, or do you feel you got lost on the way? What if you tried to reconnect with your initial promise, your inner child's voice?

It's Time to Act!

Reconnection to Your Initial Vibration

Often you lose sight of yourself, not knowing who you are, or what speaks to you anymore.

You just exist, instead of really living. To find this connection, you have to contact your true inner passion. What gets you excited? What makes you burst out laughing? Jump for joy? Literally makes you vibrate? Moves you? Gives you goose bumps?

Write down in reverse chronological order a few memories from your professional and personal life that answer these questions.

This year:

Exciting memory   Theme of this memory

_____   _____

_____   _____

_____   _____

Last year:

Exciting memory   Theme of this memory

_____   _____

_____   _____

_____   _____

The last ten (or twenty, thirty, forty, etc.) years:

Exciting memory   Theme of this memory

_____   _____

_____   _____

_____   _____

During adolescence:

      Exciting memory   Theme of this memory

_____   _____

_____   _____

_____   _____

During childhood:

      Exciting memory   Theme of this memory

_____   _____

_____   _____

_____   _____

Analyze your own evolution . . . Do you identify certain common themes or energies that show up regularly in one way or another? Now is the time to reconnect to these sensations and energies perhaps long gone.

Choose one of the activities that really excited you once, and reconnect with it, starting today.

Schedule a time in your agenda to do the same thing this weekend!

Go Further . . .

Shamanism is an interesting tool to use for exploring your inner self and connecting with your true self without mask or filter.

Start Here and Now!

Write down the first exciting memory.

**Fill your gaps,
fulfill your needs!**

FILL

What we lack instructs us.

—German proverb

If you're missing a piece, prepare a paste (*sabi-urushi*), blending the lacquer (*urushi*) with powdered stone (*tonoko*), and patiently re-create the missing piece with this paste.

Kintsugi is also the art of patiently complementing what is missing in a respectful and harmonious manner. In fact, sometimes it is even necessary to re-create the missing pieces. This is a beautiful metaphor to adopt for life: We have the choice to live unsteadily, accommodating our flaws as best we can, without trying to identify them or take care of them . . . Or, on the contrary, we can showcase them instead of denying their existence, in order to better complement them.

As I mentioned earlier, it is sometimes more difficult to detect our own flaws, which are easily visible through the eyes of others! It took me a long time to recognize my emotional voids. My initial hurt was an injury of love. Thirsty for love since my childhood, I could never get enough of it, which, ironically enough, scared and drove away others . . . When I was eight years old my best friend brutally broke up with me. I still recall the moment. She took me aside and explained to me that friendship was like a thread that sometimes breaks to attach itself to another thread. That sounds okay in theory, but the experience for me felt like a real divorce. At the time, I didn't understand why she did that. Today, with some distance, it occurs to me that she must have felt almost suffocated to take such drastic action.

For a long time, I could not see my patterns: the conditional love I was enforcing, as a mirror of my own mother's patterns ("You do not appreciate all I am doing for you"), suffocating my friends and my partners with emotional demands that were difficult to meet, unsolicited advice (savior syndrome), or inappropriately large gifts.

I remember having an epiphany during an "inner child" workshop. The host was explaining fundamental needs, and when she mentioned love, at first I did not understand. She explained that one must find love in oneself, instead of expecting it from others. It left me disconcerted. It went beyond my comprehension. It was the opposite of the way I lived! It was so incomprehensible to me, I asked her to repeat what she had said word for word so I could write it down.

I am still working on this problem, and I must admit that it is not completely solved, or I probably would not have married again, only to divorce one year after! But today I can at least see the door, the light at the end of the tunnel, and I begin to understand . . .

What about you? What are your needs? I'm not speaking of the desires that attempt to fill a vacuum (those are often of a material nature and sometimes even compulsive) but about fundamental needs, of the essential kind, often related to shortcomings from our childhood. What initial injuries do they express? Only by becoming completely cognizant of one's fundamental needs and beginning to complement what is lacking is it possible to move forward and to start to repair oneself. Fill your gaps, fulfill your needs!

The Fundamental Needs

In clearly exposing your fundamental needs, Nonviolent Communication enables you to express what is going on inside you, without blame or judgment. Messages are communicated calmly by respecting others and yourself.

The communication process in four primary phases:

❶ Objective observation and expression of concrete facts: "What I see, what I hear, what I remember . . ."

❷ Expression of emotions and feelings facing these facts: "I have the feeling . . ."

❸ Expression of needs based on underlying feelings: "Because I need . . ."

❹ Expression of a practical requirement about the actions to undertake: "I would like to . . ." "Would you agree to . . ."

This appears to be simple, but it can take a lifetime! But it is worth it, since the results are incredible.

What About You?

Do you know your basic flaws and your fundamental needs, without confusing them with desires? Do you know how to express and fulfill them?

It's Time to Act!

The Discovery of Your Needs

In his book *Words Are Windows, or They're Walls*, Marshall Rosenberg, the founder of Nonviolent Communication, established a list of fundamental needs that motivate all of us.

Grab a pen and relax. Among the following propositions, spontaneously check the key words that instinctively speak to you, without thinking too much or editing.

Autonomy

☐ Choose your dreams, your goals, your values

☐ Choose the strategies to realize your dreams, your goals, your values

Celebration

☐ Celebrate life and the realization of your dreams

☐ Celebrate your losses: loss of people close to you, the nonrealization of your dreams, etc. (mourning)

Integrity

☐ Authenticity

☐ Creativity

☐ Meaning

☐ Self-esteem

Interdependence

☐ Acceptance

☐ Appreciation

☐ Proximity

☐ Community

☐ Consideration

- [ ] Contribution to the enrichment of life
- [ ] Emotional security
- [ ] Empathy
- [ ] Honesty
- [ ] Love
- [ ] Reassurance
- [ ] Respect
- [ ] Support
- [ ] Trust
- [ ] Comprehension

Physical Nourishment

- [ ] Air
- [ ] Food
- [ ] Movement; exercise
- [ ] Protection against life-threatening organisms: viruses, bacteria, insects, predatory animals
- [ ] Rest
- [ ] Sexual Expression
- [ ] Shelter
- [ ] Touching
- [ ] Water

Play

- [ ] Amusement
- [ ] Laughter

Communion of Spirit

- [ ] Beauty
- [ ] Harmony
- [ ] Inspiration
- [ ] Order
- [ ] Peace

Copy the words you selected to page 87 (identified need), and then study the list in greater detail. These are your basic needs impacting you daily, influencing your life.

For each one, indicate if you fulfill it ("need fulfilled") or if you detect something missing ("need unfulfilled").

Wherever you have checked "need unfulfilled," imagine a way to "quench" the corresponding need by inserting a positive idea into your daily life.

For example, if you have checked "laughter" as a need, but you feel that you are not fulfilling it in your daily life, note some related activities: Reserve a seat at a comedy theater, sign up for a laughter yoga session, etc. The idea is to begin activities that complement what's lacking in your life.

Go Further . . .

On a daily basis verify with your circle of friends and family whether you express your needs to them clearly enough.

Start Here and Now!

Go to the fundamental needs list and check off all of the words that resonate in your mind.

Identified need	Need fulfilled	Need unfulfilled	Changes to make in your life
_____	☐	☐	_____
_____	☐	☐	_____
_____	☐	☐	_____
_____	☐	☐	_____
_____	☐	☐	_____
_____	☐	☐	_____
_____	☐	☐	_____

Inhale inspiration!

ASSOCIATE

Art challenges boundaries.

—Victor Hugo

If it inspires you, you can even choose a piece from another object to replace the missing piece (*yobi-tsugi*).

Sometimes the kintsugi master expands the object's transformation. Either because the flaws to repair are too severe or because of a preference for contrast, he might choose to combine two disparate objects by taking the shard of one to repair the flaw of another. Consolidated by an outside addition, the object thus becomes more original and unique, richer and more beautiful.

Here is a powerful metaphor about what the Other has to offer: Rubbing against other habits, discovering new influences and new ideas enriches our lives. Personally, I love to open myself to other cultures. For example, twelve nationalities were represented at my international business school. Most of the examinations were based on group works, which spurred us to confront different points of view and different ways of working and considerably enriched our learning. Since then I have lived and worked in France, England, Spain, and the United States (and maybe one day soon in the Netherlands). I have experimented with flying trapeze in New York; climbed a glacier in Ushuaia; performed volunteer work with handicapped children in Russia; floated in the Dead Sea in Israel and in the Red Sea in Egypt; done *la marcha* (bar tour) in Madrid and danced to techno in Belgium; climbed the 293 steps of the Tower of Pisa and the 364 steps to the top of the Statue of Liberty; eaten couscous in Tunisia and sweet herring in Denmark; drunk wine in Chile and Viennese hot chocolate in Austria; explored the fog in Oxford on bicycle, and visited the gardens of Versailles on a Segway and the canals of Amsterdam by paddleboat; toured Iceland by hitchhiking and Corsica by motorbike; participated in the Venetian carnival and the gay pride parade in Paris; teased the clown fish in the Maldives, the black squirrels at Princeton, the crocodiles in the Ivory Coast, and the whales in Madagascar—and, to crown it all, I am of Corsican origin!

It does take some effort to leave the familiar, to open oneself to others and to the world. In your own comfort zone, it appears as if there is no danger or fear. Nothing sticks out. But also, there is no challenge, nothing new, no surprises . . .

When it comes to love and relationships, for a long time I stayed in my comfort zone, searching for the perfect match with people just like me: same culture and habits, same education . . . By marrying a Moroccan-American, from a cultural background vastly different than mine, what a shift and an opening to another world! The least one can say is that it was very exotic. I had more experiences during the two years with him than during the last ten years of my life.

That is the power of cultural blending, hybrid solutions, and association mixes. By opening yourself up to the unknown, something new and different from the familiar, you are welcoming entirely new combinations, where $1 + 1 = 3$, where ideas are fused together, and where unreleased ideas are formed. So, open yourself to what is different, open your eyes and your mind, leave the beaten path you know by heart to explore new territories, let the Other enrich you. Let a breath of fresh air into your life: Inhale inspiration!

© Myriam Greff

The Beauty of Blending Cultures

At all times, cultural mixing has been a source of inspiration and richness.

In confronting different cultures, new combinations are created, unreleased and vibrant, in areas as varied as music (influence of African-American music on rock), architecture (the Arabian inspiration in Spanish architecture, the pyramid of the Louvre mixing modern and ancient styles), art (Picasso and African art, Gauguin and Tahitian art, Van Gogh and Japanese art), the culinary arts (Marco Polo's introduction of pasta to Italy upon his return from China, the European discovery of potatoes and corn imported during the exploration of the Americas, fusion food, Tex-Mex cooking), wine (vines introduced in France by the Romans), etc.

Contact with the outside can be so enriching!

What About You?

Have you always walked the same paths? And what if you were to open yourself to new inspirations and encounters outside your world?

It's Time to Act!

Open Your Mind

Are you ready to try something new? For that I suggest you play an unusual game. Pick something you do not know, something that's outside of your normal universe and, in addition, something that does not particularly tempt you because "it isn't your style!" This may appear a bit extreme, but it is the best way to get out of your own comfort zone and to let yourself be surprised.

For example:

- Go and see a film that doesn't appeal to you at all, the opposite of what you'd normally watch.

- Read a book that does not tempt you.

- Go and attend a sports event that has never interested you because it seems boring.

- Discover an exhibition you wouldn't normally attend.

- Reserve a ticket for a show that's the opposite of your usual cultural preferences.

- Go to a restaurant you don't know to order food you don't particularly think you'll enjoy.

- Watch a TV program or series that doesn't appeal to you.

- Dress in a style completely different from what you normally wear.

- Listen to a style of music that you don't like.

Let yourself be surprised and carried away!

Go Further . . .

If you liked this exercise, extend it to an entire weekend to let yourself be surprised in all areas.

Start Here and Now!

Quickly choose one of the listed activities! (And yes, certainly one of those that tempts you the least!)

STAGE 3

WAIT

霧時雨富士を見ぬ日ぞ面白き

Kiri shigure / Fuji o minu hi zo / omoshiroki

———

Chilling autumn rains
curtain Mount Fuji, then make it
more beautiful to see.

Matsuo Bashō
(1644–1694)

Return to your true essence.

REMOVE

Perfection is achieved, not when there is nothing more to add, but when there is nothing more to take away.

—Antoine de Saint-Exupéry

Scrape off the extra matter with a utensil (razor blade, toothpick, palette knife), and clean using turpentine.

This step is very important. When assembling the pieces to be fused together, some glue will seep out of the fissures. It's therefore essential to take the time to remove any excess matter with care, because once it has hardened, it compromises the remaining repair.

Just like in life, to move forward with ease, it's necessary to take one's time to get rid of superfluous, encumbering matter, whether it's of a physical or mental nature.

Often, while consumed by the chaos of daily life, it's difficult to clearly see your priorities. The superfluous constantly threatens the essential. Always wanting to accumulate more, you try to do too much and end up saturated and overloaded.

Ironically, even when trying to discover your well-being, you can find yourself out of breath and exhausted. At the beginning of my spiritual quest, I wanted to try a bunch of different things at the same time: all the methods, all the books, all the seminars, and all the conferences—from one extreme to the other. I didn't have much spare time, but I ran from one lecture to another, from one meeting to the next. In addition, I was trying to manage my life as a young single mother, my wedding planning business, my swing dancing lessons, and my physical and mental personal-development training. One day I arrived at the office of an energy therapist literally running, out of breath and out of steam. How relaxing . . . How can you possibly hope to find your balance in such a state of chaos? How can you take the time to assimilate the notions you've learned if you're always running from one learning process to another?

With all of this accumulation, I had to learn how to simplify, to sort, to remove the excess, and to keep only the essential. No matter what your excess stuff might be, whether it is materialistic (too much shopping, accumulated objects, expenses), physical (too many pounds), or mental (too much responsibility, too many obligations, even too many hobbies), it becomes necessary to reduce it in order to see clearly what's going on. Remove everything that holds you down and weighs heavily on your mind and body: refine, purify, simplify your life. Return to your true essence.

© Myriam Greff

The Big Stones Metaphor

This parable explains the importance of differentiating between the superfluous and the essential . . .

One day, an old professor at one of the great business schools taught his students this masterful lesson about life.

He placed a big, empty jar on his desk. Then he put six large stones into the jar until they came up to the rim. He asked his students, "Is this jar full now?" The students all together answered "Yes!" "Are you sure about that?" responded the professor. Then he took a handful of gravel and put in the jar. "And now, do you think the jar is full?" he continued. The students once again said yes. The professor added a handful of sand. "And now?" Now, less sure of themselves, the students answered hesitantly, "Yes, the jar is now full after all." Finally, the professor emptied a bowl of water into the jar and said, "Now it's full. This jar represents your life and the manner in which you manage your time. Tell me the hidden metaphor behind this story!" One of the students dared to come forward with a guess. "Even when you think you don't have any more time, there's always more space to introduce something else into your plan!"

The old professor answered, "More importantly, it illustrates the need to identify what matters the most in your life. The big stones represent your priorities, the things you deem essential. Often you tend to focus on small urgencies, the minor things that catch your attention, as represented by the gravel, the sand, and the water. If I had put them into the jar first, there would have been no room for the larger stones. Concentrate first on your own large stones; put them first in the jar of your life and make sure they fit. Do you know what your large stones are?"

What About You?

What matters the most in your life? What heavy obligations do you impose upon yourself? What do you accumulate? Excess pounds? Debt? Objects? Memories? Guilt? Procrastination? And what if you started to lighten the load?

It's Time to Act!

The Great Sorting

The time has come to lighten your load in every sense of the word. After all, it makes sense that books about organizing, arranging, and zero waste are so popular: Our environment impacts our mind and our inner self.

List what weighs you down:

_____

_____

_____

_____

_____

To evolve in life, make it a priority to release yourself from this weight.

Go Further . . .

The scope of this task seems overwhelming. That's logical, because it's exactly what is weighing you down. It appears to be an insurmountable mountain.

But a mountain can be climbed in smaller, easier stages, one step after the other.

The secret of attacking such an objective lies in simplifying and breaking it down, task by task, into smaller actions that aren't so scary and don't require more than five minutes. The most difficult task is getting started: Program an alarm for five minutes. Once you've taken the first step, you may be eager to continue with the next . . .

Task to accomplish	Break it down	Further simplify each action

For example, losing sixty pounds may seem insurmountable. "So what's the point, I might as well have another piece of cake . . . what's a little more or a little less . . ." Therefore the objective to note is not "sixty pounds" but to break it down to "one pound," which is way more feasible.

Or if you've never sorted through your paperwork, it appears impossible for you to attack a massive lifetime of papers. "So what's the point? It's just as well to add today's mail to the top of the pile. What's a little more or a little less . . ." Therefore the task at hand isn't "sorting through all of the paperwork," but the first step is to create a file for the phone bills.

Start Here and Now!

Take the first, smallest step on your list: Organize your sock drawer, send that e-mail you've avoided sending for the last six months, call the plumber, or cancel the meeting that overburdens your day . . .

Start a new habit,
start a new life!

MAINTAIN

Great works are performed not by strength, but by perseverance.

—Samuel Johnson

Make sure the pieces stay in place by wrapping the object with masking tape or rubber bands.

Once the cleaning has been accomplished, it's important to keep the pieces firmly attached to each other, so that they remain perfectly welded together during the drying phase. Once dry, the object will be more solid.

In life it's also important to maintain a certain structure, so that the changes you've initiated have time to take hold, to become part of your day-to-day routine, until they are solid.

It took me quite a while to understand this. With my go-getter and bulldozer nature, once I made a positive resolution, I wanted to change everything at the same time. For example, with my legendary enthusiasm, I might have decided to start jogging, do yoga, get up every morning at six o'clock in order to start my "Miracle Morning," put lotion on my body regularly, meditate for forty minutes and visualize my day, sort through my entire cabinet, do my spring cleaning, and, of course, everything else I could think of . . . all on the same day. I would thus prepare a meticulous, step-by-step plan of action, which I would stick to perfectly . . . for only the first five days. Obviously, it was impossible to keep up this routine for any longer length of time, because there were too many changes all at once.

Today I understand that the requirement for keeping up with change is to concentrate on one task only, giving it the necessary time to blend into your life. Some speak of twenty-one days. For me it takes about a month before a new habit instills itself seamlessly into my life. It's the time the brain needs to install new patterns so that the new habit becomes a well-grounded, automatic reflex, like brushing your teeth!

Since it's impossible to change everything at the same time, you have to focus on a single habit. When you're really motivated, one habit at a time might seem like too little and maybe even too slow! But when you think about it, starting a new habit per month creates twelve new habits per year! And that's huge, particularly once they're all well ingrained.

So, concentrate all of your efforts on a unique objective, and maintain that attention for at least one month. Start a new habit, start a new life!

Neuroplasticity

In order to maintain a good habit, it's necessary to give the brain time to create new "pathways." In fact, the human brain is a marvel of perfection that trains itself to accomplish repetitive tasks so we can adapt to our environment and learn better.

This malleability of the brain is due to the plasticity of neurons, which can create new synaptic connections, like creating new roads to connect different towns. A little like how an often-used path is well marked and a path seldom used becomes overgrown, so too our neurons, if used regularly, can build "highways."

The anatomy of the brain therefore evolves as a result of this learning and these new habits. Some areas of the brain can be reactivated, even regenerating themselves! And the good news is that the brain remains malleable no matter how old we are.

What About You?

Do you have a tendency to change everything at once when you're motivated but get discouraged just a few days afterward? What if you choose a single objective to concentrate on with all of your strength and energy?

It's Time to Act!

The Twelve Habits

Which habits would you like to integrate into your life? For example, these might include small changes (such as brushing your teeth three times a day, backing up your work regularly, cleaning the dishes after meals, or taking care of your skin twice a week). Or they might be more demanding (such as meditating for twenty minutes per day, getting up an hour earlier every morning, stopping watching a TV series, going jogging three times a week, or using the stairs instead of the elevator).

❶ List them all, no matter whether they're easy or more demanding, without sorting them out, a bit like new year's resolutions. It's important to formulate them into precise actions. For example, write down "stop buying cake" instead of "lose weight."

❷ Circle the twelve activities that appear to be the most important to you.

❸ Sort them from the easiest to the most demanding.

❹ Allow one month for each, and start today with the easiest.

Month of _____ Habit #1: _____

Month of _____ Habit #2: _____

Month of _____ Habit #3: _____

Month of _____ Habit #4: _____

Month of _____ Habit #5: _____

Month of _____ Habit #6: _____

Month of _____ Habit #7: _____

Month of _____ Habit #8: _____

Month of _____ Habit #9: _____

Month of _____ Habit #10: _____

Month of _____ Habit #11: _____

Month of _____ Habit #12: _____

❺ And there you have your program for the coming year!

Go Further . . .

If you need help to get motivated, show the list to a good friend who can help guide you during the entire year.

Start Here and Now!

Write down your first habit.

Take a break,
take a breath!

BREATHE

I have so much to accomplish today that I must meditate for two hours instead of one.

—Gandhi

The lacquer (*urushi*) is alive and needs to breathe to dry and to harden. Prepare a covered cardboard box (*muro*), and place a damp towel in the bottom. Using a number of wooden sticks, create a grid so the object can be placed on it.

The lacquer has the rare capacity to breathe, almost like a living creature! Extracted from the sap of a tree, it injects a second life into the object, thus helping cure it. Therefore, like all living organisms, it needs to breathe. The lacquer absorbs oxygen and humidity while it continues to breathe during the long process of curing. As the lacquer slowly hardens, it makes the object increasingly more resilient over the months.

This phase reminds us how vital it is to take your time if you do not want to be short of breath in the course of any kind of healing procedure.

As a young entrepreneur, while managing a particularly exhausting wedding planning business and dashing around at one hundred miles per hour, I never took the time during the day to stop, even for just a few minutes. I was extremely efficient and productive . . . Or, at least I thought I was. Today I know that taking breaks throughout the day reduces stress and improves creativity and overall performance.

Certain studies even consider the ideal daily rhythm to consist of seventeen minutes of pausing for every fifty-two minutes of activity.

Without going that far, I invite you to learn how to breathe regularly throughout your day by using one of the following techniques: resonant breathing, yoga, afternoon nap, meditation, abdominal respiration, sport, etc. This is particularly important, especially when you don't have the time. Personally, I allow myself a meditation session after lunch and regularly pause throughout the day to prepare myself rosebud tea. I also run three times per week.

By breathing regularly, even when stressed, we send a message of relaxation and serenity to the brain. We thereby change its frequency and help to progressively reprogram it. Often during times of intense stress, you get short of breath, with a tightness in the chest. A baby, on the other hand, sleeps peacefully, breathing with its belly. So don't forget to take a break, take a breath!

Resonant Breathing

If you breathe regularly in a constant rhythm, your breathing aligns itself with the rhythm of your heartbeat, thus sending a message of relaxation and stress reduction to your brain.

In fact, an obvious link between the brain and the heart exists: When stressed, the heart has the tendency to beat faster and irregularly. By breathing calmly, you obtain a more regular cardiac frequency, which transmits information of well-being directly to the brain.

To start with, it's often recommended to use the daily method of "3-6-5":

- 3 times per day

- 6 respiration cycles per minute

- 5 minutes in a row

Start by first getting calm and taking a deep abdominal breath through your nose for five seconds (letting your stomach inflate), and then exhale deeply through your mouth for five seconds (deflating your stomach), and go on like this for five minutes.

Many applications or videos show how to familiarize yourself with this resonant breathing method, with or without music. Try it. It's quite simple and its impact can be felt instantly.

What About You?

Do you take the time to regularly take a break during the day? What if you paused to catch your breath?

It's Time to Act!

Daily Breaks for Breathing

In order to manage regular breathing space throughout the day, choose one of the following techniques:

- Resonant breathing
- Mindfulness meditation
- Yoga
- Running
- Sport
- Abdominal respiration
- Afternoon nap
- Sophrology
- Guided meditation

Now program an alarm (for example, to do abdominal breathing for one minute every hour, or for resonant breathing three times a day), or use an already existing time that's easy to remember (brushing your teeth, after lunch, every Wednesday, during traffic jams) to catch your breath.

Go Further . . .

Have you tried forest bathing? For some time this practice (*Shinrin-yoku*) had been forgotten, but it was reintroduced by Japanese doctors during the 1980s, and today it's quite popular again for its many benefits for the body and mind. Walking outside in nature, breathing air that is naturally rich in essential oils, helps oxygenate our brain and body cells, effectively reduces stress, controls mood swings, reduces heart rate, and strengthens the lungs and muscles.

Start Here and Now!

Take a break and take a breath now!

Ready, set . . . rest.

PAUSE

Let us allow our minds a few moments of calm each day. The most beautiful fruit of the soul: peace, joy, and tenderness, are born of this deep silence.

—Frédéric Lenoir

The lacquer hardens best at a humidity level of 75 to 90 percent and at a temperature above 68°F. Place the object in this box, maintaining constant temperature and humidity levels.

The time has come to place the object in the box to settle. In life too, it's often necessary to stop for a moment. Once in the midst of an activity, it's often difficult to know when to stop. But just as it's necessary for land to lie barren in a fallow period for a time to regenerate, it's necessary to manage one's time and pause while battling those self-imposed challenges. Henceforth, it is necessary to lower our defenses so we can recharge.

And yet, for a long time I believed that action was the answer! Always faster, always further . . . Cutting back on my sleep, even my hobbies were timed! But sometimes it's necessary to let things settle in order to see more clearly. To let your subconscious work at its own pace and absorb new thoughts. Today I am gradually learning to slow down and ease my mind, warm and wrapped up in Danish hygge style: taking time for breakfast in bed, relaxing contentedly in front of a fire with a good book, contemplating a burning candle, and savoring a delicious cup of tea.

You too can create comforting rituals. Take good care of yourself. After all of your efforts, all of your battles, all of your progress, you certainly deserve a break! Ready, set . . . rest.

The Japanese Tea Ceremony

This is the ideal moment to mention the traditional Japanese tea ceremony. Sometimes it takes an entire lifetime to fully understand the stylized and contemplative nature of this ceremony or to appreciate all the precise gestures of the tea master and his guests. Highly symbolic, this is not about just the preparation of a beverage but rather the search for harmony, respect, purity, and serenity (*wa, kei, sei, jaku*).

In Japan, where this ritual can be traced back to the twelfth century, it is called *chanoyu*, literally meaning "hot water for tea." The actual art of the tea ceremony is called *chado*, "the Way of Tea," and is considered one of the ways to reach serenity, as tea is a symbol of awakening in every sense of the word.

The tea ceremony requires simple accessories of modest beauty made from natural materials. These elements invite participants to contemplate and appreciate their imperfections and remind guests of all the flaws in human nature, echoing the philosophy of kintsugi.

What About You?

Do you know how to slow down? What if you took the time to gently settle down from time to time?

It's Time to Act!

The Infusion

Take the time to slowly settle down and prepare your own personal tea ceremony. Taking time to care for yourself is an integral part of the curing process.

The preparation is an important part of the ritual. Choose a special tea, with the kind of fragrance and flavor that takes you away. The exercise can also be executed with a delicate herbal tea or an excellent coffee, based on your personal preference. Personally, I often choose white tea delicately flavored with lychee, rose petals, and apricot.

Choose a piece of beautiful porcelain, but not just any piece: This should be a cup or bowl that has a significant, symbolic value to you. I use a square cup from the eighteenth century given to me by a friend on my fortieth birthday, a cup I have "kintsugied." Refined, original, and a bit askew with its cracks covered in gold, it represents me perfectly!

Mindfully prepare the infusion with pure water, watching the tea or the brewing coffee defuse slowly, drop by drop. Savor each sip of this nectar slowly, mindfully, and with gratitude . . . Finally, thank yourself for having taken the time to take care of yourself and to infuse yourself with a healing spirit.

Go Further . . .

Arrange for a special time with yourself, for instance every Sunday. After a number of weeks, the flavor of your beverage will take you away instantly, like Marcel Proust's madeleine.

Start Here and Now!

Right now, choose the tea and the cup.

Wash your heart,
wash your life!

CLEAN

A change of the exterior circumstances of our life only works through the transformation of our body.

—Emmet Fox

Carefully clean your tools (palette knife, palettes, brushes) after each stage with turpentine or vegetable oil, and carefully organize them so they are ready for the next use.

This step is neither the most attractive nor terribly creative. And yet it's an integral part of the entire process; it's as indispensable as all the others.

Just as the kintsugi master cleans his material mindfully and with respect, be sure to take care of your body along with your mind during the healing process. It's time for the big spring cleaning! Whether it's cleansing your insides, your outside, or even your spirit, the time has come to shake up old, stagnating energies. Spark these into motion to get rid of the dead skin that's associated with your past. You are not the same person any longer. It's time for the shedding!

During an important transition in my life, I personally feel the need to take care of my body: sometimes through a massage, or a stay at a spa, or by fasting for a week. I clean my body (and my mind) to facilitate the emergence of the new me.

As expressed by Dr. Catherine Kousmine, "Your body is a temple." Treat it like the sacred temple it is. And then she adds, "Don't let just anything be brought inside of it!"

Experiment with the techniques you prefer: Rub, thin, cleanse, move, sweat, mobilize, evacuate, brush, scrub, or massage. *Inochi no sentaku, kokoro no sentaku* (literally, "washing life, washing heart" in Japanese). So let go of what needs to go, make a fresh start, and wash your heart, wash your life!

Baths of the World

Multiple cultures on this planet explore the benefits of steam and heat. No matter where, bathing has similar characteristics in different countries. The contrast of hot and cold, the dilating effect of heat, the benefits of essential oils, and relaxing with steam are universal, impacting the body (by softening the skin, strengthening the heart, stimulating blood circulation, evacuating toxins, relieving muscle soreness, facilitating breathing, reinforcing immune defenses) as well as the mind (relaxing, reducing stress, aiding sleep, improving conviviality, and sharing an intimate moment).

I have personally had the most incredible experience deep in the Ural Mountains, at the invitation of a Russian friend, to try out the *banya* (Russian bath) in an authentic dacha (Russian country home) in the Yekaterinburg countryside. It was a surreal scene where I found myself in a small, wooden cabin in the middle of nowhere. After sweating, I was surprised by a whipping with birch branches to help the blood circulate! Fortunately, this took place during the summer, so I was spared a roll in the snow. It was very stimulating!

In Japan too, the tradition of bathing is very important. Since ancient times, the Japanese people have used hot springs (*onsens*) to relax with friends and family and to cleanse their bodies and minds. In fact the custom is to wash oneself before entering the hot bath, so you can concentrate on relaxing and sharing. Symbolically, the Japanese bath is intended to dissolve your sorrows in the hot water and to wash your heart, wash your life!

What About You?

Do you take care of your body as a sacred temple? What if you treated it as it deserves, so that new energies emerge?

It's Time to Act!

The Big Spring Cleaning

There are so many techniques for cleaning your body . . . Here is just a brief overview to inspire you. Which one(s) would you like to try?

Exterior body cleaning: sport (to sweat), hammam, hydrotherapy, Swedish sauna, Russian baths, Japanese baths, scrubbing, dry brushing, lymphatic draining, thalassotherapy, etc.

Interior body cleansing: colon cleansing, fasting, grape cure, mono-diet, liver detox, etc.

Energy cleansing: Chinese belly massage (*chi nei tsang*), acupuncture, fasciatherapy, micro-physiotherapy, Japanese shiatsu, Reiki, etc.

Go Further . . .

Read, explore, look at videos, search the Internet, and educate yourself if you would like to acquire a deeper knowledge of these subjects.

Start Here and Now!

Pick up your phone and immediately set up your first appointment.

It's time
to let time
do its work.

REST

How poor are they that have not patience! What wound did ever heal but by degrees?

—William Shakespeare

Patiently leave the object in the box for seven to ten days, until it has dried.

Kintsugi is a veritable education in patience and deliberation. Impatiently, we may want to move immediately to the key phase of covering the lacquered fissures with gold powder, to admire the object emerged in new splendor. But the art of kintsugi reminds us that it isn't the outcome that counts but the way we get there . . . Kintsugi values slowness, inviting us to wait until the object's cracks have completely dried and healed for fear of it breaking again if we are too impatient.

All of this waiting is part of the object's repair and regeneration, just as in life patience facilitates the healing process. Take the required time. Or rather, give yourself the time you need. Certainly, you would love for things to go faster! But you need to humbly accept the time it takes and beware of quick solutions that are often superficial. To really heal to the depth of your soul, you can't touch a fresh scar too soon without risking that it will reopen or perhaps even get infected.

To be honest, patience does not come easily to me. Rather, I am the type of person who pulls on the leaves of a plant to make it grow faster! All my life I've had the tendency to make fast decisions. Overnight, I quit my dream job in the fragrance industry. In three days, I decided to start my wedding planning business with no backup plan. In a second, I made the decision to get a divorce when the truth was unveiled. In four hours, just after my mother committed suicide, I shut down the company I had owned for ten years. I regret none of these decisions, but the least one can say is that patience is not one of my strengths!

And yet, when I first discovered kintsugi, it was love at first sight, immediate and unconditional. I had the impression of having finally found my *Ikigai*, my reason for being. And that, in spite of requiring much effort, concentration, attention to detail, and patience, it was worth it. Initially all that interested me was the final result—the object covered in gold. But soon I discovered all the necessary stages. And to my great surprise, I started to enjoy experiencing every one of them. Even waiting out the time for drying, I eventually learned to let go. Many times I even had to start the whole process over again as a result of a hurried gesture or heavy application with the brush, or when the entire puzzle of pieces broke again at the very moment when I was ready to let it finally dry!

The spirit of kintsugi is becoming a part of me. Waiting is no longer so painful. I am learning to let a decision mature by taking my time to appreciate the path. Incidentally, my oldest daughter is very contemplative and is not always as fast and as efficient as I would like her to be . . . Just like a kintsugi master (and aren't our children our masters?), she has taught me to slow down, reminding me every day that slowness isn't a fault.

You too should take the time to turn a page. Savor the wait, appreciate slowness, and enjoy every passing second that brings you closer to your cure: It's time to let time do its work.

Zen Walking Meditation

Walking is always an excellent way to unite body and mind. Many important thinkers have had epiphanies while walking! The Zen walk (*kinhin* means "instructed walking") proposes a walking practice of meditation. Based on Japanese Zen Buddhist practice, it attempts to harmonize steps with breathing. By advancing at the rhythm of respiration, the walker automatically slows down in order to avoid forced breathing.

In practice this means walking with a straight back, looking at the ground rather than far ahead, keeping one's eyes half closed, and holding one's hands in *shashu* (left fist closed around the thumb, with right hand covering the left fist). Breathing in, one mindfully advances a half step, slowly, silently aware. When breathing out, the two hands should be one against the other so that the base of the left thumb pushes against the solar plexus. Then one breathes in again, taking another half step with the other leg.

Kinhin is Zen in action, moving forward "like a tiger in the jungle or a serpent in the sea." One turns inward to progressively develop stability, concentration, being in control of oneself and one's energy.

What About You?

Do you have the patience and wisdom to let time do its work? Or are you the type that pulls on the leaves of the plant to make it grow faster? What might happen if you were to slow down a bit?

It's Time to Act!

The Art of Patience

Do you sometimes have the tendency to hurry unnecessarily? To respond, note all the moments of your life during which you have made hurried decisions, wanting to advance a bit too fast.

_____

_____

_____

_____

_____

_____

_____

_____

_____

_____

_____

_____

_____

_____

_____

_____

Go Further . . .

Since mindfulness learning can pass through the entire body, take a slow Zen walking meditation (*kinhin*) or a *chi gong* session to literally incorporate into all of your cells this new sensation of slowness.

Start Here and Now!

Slow down your gestures, walk slowly and mindfully, savor the path with mindfulness.

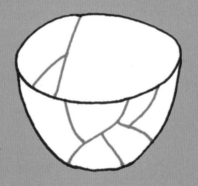

STAGE 4

REPAIR

七転び八起き

nanakorobi yaoki

———

Fall down seven times, get up eight.

—Japanese proverb

Smooth your soul.

POLISH

The gem cannot be polished without friction,
nor a man perfected without trials.

—Chinese proverb

Once the object is perfectly dry, clean the excess matter with a scraper and turpentine. Then use sandpaper to completely smooth out the surface. What remain on the object now are nothing but brown scars (*urushi-tsugi*).

When the glue is dry, the time has come to gently remove the excess with sandpaper by polishing the cracks until they are smooth, as if they have blended into the object's surface. They are visible to the eye but indiscernible to the touch. The cracks have been filled but are still healing: Many steps remain before the object can rediscover with pride its true self and new beauty. However, the object is now whole and reconnected.

This is a beautiful metaphor for the approach to healing and personal development. Gradually we polish our thoughts, memories, traumas, beliefs, and feelings until there is no more pain and anger. Bit by bit, we remove the layers of emotion protecting ourselves not only from others but also from ourselves. Slowly we recognize the very heart of being our true self. This can be quite unnerving at first. Our reflexes are conditioned to trigger automatic emotional responses that have served as the core of our being for many years. Our heart is unprotected. But maybe, for the first time in a long time, we are true to ourselves, real, exposed.

It's now time to remove your mask and reveal what's hidden beneath it.

When I removed my first, outermost, protective layer containing the mask of the all-is-well, nice, smiling person, I did expose a layer of sadness beneath. Since this sadness had surfaced several times before, I wasn't too surprised. Consequently, during the years of my personal development, I worked a lot on this particular emotion. But through polishing even more, I was surprised to find yet another layer that was hidden deeper and more rooted: an intense anger that boiled out of me like fire from a dragon! As more and more anger spilled out of me, drop by drop, I started to clean up this venom. Today, I continue to polish and polish more, removing one layer each time. I progress, I take two steps forward then one back, I get up again, I try to improve . . . I know that someday I will get there. I look forward to discovering what is hidden under this anger layer!

Like water that polishes pebbles, drop by drop, over thousands of years and that can drill holes through rocks, the emotional and psychological polishing is a long process, sometimes lasting an entire lifetime. But do you have anything better to do than to improve yourself?

One by one, drop by drop, layer by layer, gently polish your problems until you have revealed your original self. Smooth your soul.

Suiseki, or the Beauty of Polished Stones

Suiseki, a Japanese term meaning "stone worked by water," is an ancient Japanese art form consisting of a collection of the most beautiful stones found in nature. These stones have been sculpted by water, wind, and time into beautiful shapes: a landscape, a mountain, an animal, a plant, or an abstract form.

With their natural beauty, without any intervention other than the creation of a tailor-made wooden stand, these natural masterpieces are fashioned by thousands of years. They are an expression of stability, patience, and simplicity, reminding us to humbly contemplate nature and the passing of time.

What About You?

Do you sometimes hide below the layers of your shell? What if you tried to polish them one by one to reveal your true self?

It's Time to Act!

The Potter's Wheel

Try this visualization to support you in your healing path.

Get settled in a calm and quiet location, turn off your phone, and isolate yourself for a few minutes from the rest of the world.

Imagine a potter's wheel in front of you. If you're having trouble visualizing it, take a look at a short video or the famous scene in the film *Ghost*!

Now place the lump of clay that represents you, including all of the problems you'd like to work on, on the wheel. Whatever ails you, hurts you, or makes you suffer.

Contemplate the details of the formless mass in all of its roughness.

Imagine centering the mass on the wheel, putting yourself symbolically in the center.

Now pour a glass of water over the clay, representing the purification and care you're applying to yourself.

Carefully put your hands on the clay. Connect with its vitality.

Let the energy of healing enter through your hands.

Take the clay into your hands and mentally start to turn the wheel.

Let your hands slide over the clay from top to bottom. Feel the sensations that result: Imagine the matter gliding through your hands, the odor of the clay mixed with water, the whirring of the wheel, the hypnotic turning of the object you're trying to shape.

Make a hole in the center using your thumbs. This represents your willingness to get to the heart of the problem.

Now shape the object. What does it represent? Maybe an abstract form, a vase, a bowl, a plate, or a ball?

Feel how the mass is now soft and smooth.

How many of its bumps you have polished away . . .

Observe your body's reaction. Do you feel relaxed? Are there still parts on you that are tight or clenched? If so, just continue to polish a bit longer, until you find yourself in harmony.

Virtually remove the object from the wheel, passing a wire under the object, cutting the clay, indicating to your subconscious the willingness to move to another stage in your life.

Put the object in a symbolic location representing well-being to you.

Admire the object regularly in your thoughts. Connect yourself to this creation when you start rethinking the initial problem, in order to reconnect with the feeling of wellness now rooted deep inside you.

Decorate it so you can celebrate your rebirth and your healing.

Go Further . . .

Repeat this exercise in real life by taking a pottery course.

Start Here and Now!

Get settled comfortably and begin the visualization.

Let yourself be touched . . .

TOUCH

*There is nothing better than a look
and a touch to know where one is.*

—Tahar Ben Jelloun

It is sometimes difficult to recognize certain irregularities with the naked eye. Using your fingers and sense of touch, verify that all the joints are perfectly smooth.

As in the art of kintsugi, in life the sense of touch is indispensable to one's balance and well-being. For instance, studies have shown that money left by accident is more likely to be returned if the person who found the money is lightly touched on the shoulder when asked for it. Other studies have shown that infants born prematurely who receive extra care and massage, or who sleep on warm, lambskin rugs develop much faster than the babies in the control group.

Even if it's difficult to measure precisely and quantify the results of such studies, could it be that what is true for newborn babies also applies to us? Wouldn't our bodies be starved for the sense of touch in a society where everything is dematerialized and physical contact is reduced for fear of being misunderstood as harassment? Wouldn't we miss a touch of gentleness in a brutal world?

Along these lines, there are two tendencies that have emerged: free hugs, almost anywhere in the world, offered by complete strangers without any afterthoughts or sexual connotation; and lately, hugging bars coming from Japan.

After my divorce, my naturopath prescribed regular massages to rediscover the physical limits of my body and my sensory stimuli. I therefore recommend regular massages and touching, because the tactile contact is vital for your equilibrium. The sense of touch is often associated with sensuality and sexuality, but that is a very limited interpretation: It seems to me that it has a much wider role to play. After all, many therapies base their treatments on the sense of touch. I have tried one of these that is rather unknown, the "clay block" method, which permits us to reconnect to our inner depth by touching the soil.

In order to get used to and to rehabilitate your everyday sense of touch, to get back your sensory stimuli, and to increase your good vibrations, surround yourself with smoothness, silky cream, and soft textiles; massage yourself; cuddle people around you; take somebody into your arms, and tickle and hug them; pat an animal; make love; dance in the arms of somebody . . .

Improving your sense of touch will enhance your mental and physical balance. Renew contact with yourself, let yourself be touched . . .

Shiatsu

Japanese massage is called shiatsu, meaning "finger pressure."

It's recognized by the Japanese Health Ministry as a therapeutic technique utilizing fingers and the palms of the hands to apply pressure to certain well-determined body parts. It is practiced while fully dressed, without use of any oils. It concentrates on acupuncture points and body meridians, to circulate blocked energy.

Stimulating and eliminating tension and muscle spasms, based on the theory of yin and yang, the two opposite yet complementary energy centers, shiatsu visualizes human health in its wholeness: physical, psychological, and spiritual.

What About You?

Do you have enough tactile contact every day? What if you reconnected with yourself with hugs, touch, massage, and cuddles?

It's Time to Act!

Massage Therapy

What if, step by step, you were to bring back the sense of touch to your body?

Swedish, Californian, Ayurvedic, Korean or Thai, Fasciatherapy, shiatsu or Japanese sitting *amma* therapy, foot or palm reflexology, auto massage, among friends or family or with a professional, with or without oil, upright, sitting or lying down, naked or dressed, relaxing or stimulating—there are innumerable massage techniques. Try out a few and find the best one for you.

Go Further . . .

Develop your tactile sense of touch on a daily basis by offering free hugs to the people around you, and why not to strangers? Cultivate the habit of lightly (without ambiguity) touching the person in front of you.

Start Here and Now!

Make an appointment for a massage, or massage your own neck and feet.

The only right
moment is now!

APPLY

The world is full of good intentions,
what is lacking is to apply them.

—Blaise Pascal

With a small brush apply a first layer of black lacquer (*roiro-urushi*) to all the joints.

By concentrating on applying a thin layer, the kintsugi master prepares the object for the following steps. The cracks are thus completely smoothed out, ready to receive the final layer: The repair can proceed harmoniously.

Life also invites you to begin all of your activities harmoniously with a fine layer of good principles. Don't leave them on the road of good intentions. Even with the strongest resolution in mind, it's sometimes difficult to put this into practice. And the worst part is that we have the tendency to procrastinate with the execution of what is most important! "I start tomorrow." "I am getting ready." "I will begin after vacation." Do these remind you of someone? By procrastinating for the longest time possible, you water down your intentions until they become completely out of sight. Every missed opportunity distances you from your goal and from your real self.

I have to admit that I have fallen into this trap, like many others. When I first discovered kintsugi, it was love at first sight, a real revelation! Of course I researched the subject, but I didn't dare begin my first repairs, because I was intimidated by the complexity of this art. In addition, I felt deep inside that this was a serious step from which there might be no return.

141

So I remained shyly at the edge of the swimming pool, testing the temperature of the water with my toes . . . What a delight and what a pleasure when I finally stopped procrastinating and dived right into the techniques! It felt like discovering long-lost ancestral gestures buried deep within myself. I, the impatient bulldozer, took pleasure in preparing the materials and assembling the puzzles. Sometimes, after hours of work, the repaired piece would break again, but then I patiently started again, without any rush or frustration. I even learned to enjoy the wait!

I am mentioning it simply to remind you that the first step is often the most difficult part. We are all a bit like a tank, difficult to start moving but advancing straight for our target once we get going. We must fight this tendency toward inertia and act now. The smallest action is more valuable than the longest speech! It's not the theory that counts but the execution. It seems there are three things most successful people have in common: They meditate, they get up early, and they floss! Intriguing, isn't it? Obviously, it's not that dental floss is a key to success, but if one is sufficiently disciplined to use it every day, the same discipline can be applied to other activities . . . What about you? Do you floss?

One day . . . later . . . too late! The only right moment is now! In a year from now, you'll wish that you had started today. So shift into a higher gear and execute your plan of action!

The Miracle Morning

This book by Hal Elrod is a true bestseller, improving life for millions of people. It's extremely motivating, proposing a morning plan of action to finally work on everything you have the tendency to postpone. You start early in the day to tackle the principal tasks you've identified for yourself. In this manner . . .

- They automatically become part of your daily program.

- You finally put your good principles into action.

- You start on the right foot, generating enough energy for the remainder of the day.

Everybody is free to determine his own morning program. For example, the author proposes six "life SAVERS" steps: S stands for Silence (meditation, prayer, gratitude, respiration), A for Affirmation (motivating phrases about what you really desire to program your subconscious), V for Visualization (visualize your objectives), E for Exercise (sport, gymnastics, abs, stretching, yoga), R for Reading (read a book about personal development, an inspiring work, a collection of motivational citations), and S for Scribing (notes in your journal, personal action plan, reflections about life).

Personally, I start with a quick morning wash to wake up, including my Ayurvedic oil detox mouthwash and a tongue scraper. (This only takes ten minutes, and to save time, I take my shower the evening before.) Then I continue with a twenty-five-minute yoga session. After that I sit down on a meditation pillow for five minutes of mindfulness, two minutes for my affirmations, two minutes to visit my inner child, three minutes for my objectives, three minutes for a fast body scan to check whether there is anything blocked, one minute to verify my energy level, twenty minutes to sit comfortably on my bed reading a book on personal development, and five minutes to enter a few notes in my journal.

At this point our little household wakes up. I continue my miracle morning with the famous organic and vegan Budwig cream by Dr. Kousmine, an essential recipe I couldn't live without, my six spirulina pills, and my morning drink, a big mug (two cups) of lukewarm water (according to Ayurvedic principles) filtered by reverse osmosis, to which I add an organic rosebud.

No need for coffee or tea: Regaining energy is quite fabulous! It's just a habit to adopt. After a month it becomes easy. By carefully preparing for this "miracle," one feels the same excitement a child does on Christmas Eve, ready to unwrap the presents of one's life.

What About You?

Are you disciplined in your daily life or are you a procrastinator? What life-changing good ideas should you be following? What if you started by applying the first one, here and now?

It's Time to Act!

The Application

No need to listen to long speeches. The time has come to put theory into practice! Stop reading and immediately implement one of the things you have postponed for a long time.

Act on that good advice in your head, take that step you've postponed, send that tedious e-mail, make that difficult phone call, send that late invoice, go to the meeting you have canceled twice. In two words, start now!

Go Further . . .

Start every day with a task you normally put off. By tackling it with a clear morning mind, you will finally begin to act.

To accomplish this, write down the morning task on a sticky note the night before and put it on your desk in plain view. You are programming your brain and your subconscious, preparing yourself psychologically. In the morning, you can't forget, and you've programmed yourself not to delay this task any longer. Remember this wonderful sensation and the relief you feel when you've finally accomplished a task that you postponed for months . . .

Start Here and Now!

Really? Are you still reading now instead of starting?

Centered and concentrated.

CONCENTRATE

For each moment of our lives is essentially irreplaceable; you should learn to sink yourself in it utterly.

—André Gide

Breathe calmly, concentrate, and execute slowly, using measured and precise gestures to apply thin lines to the joints. Let this first application dry in the box for one to two weeks.

Like a calligrapher, the kintsugi master measures every one of his gestures, perfect, fine, and precise, to cover each line of the broken object. This is an important phase. If the layer is too thick, it dries in a coarse manner, ruining the surface. He, therefore, has to be completely centered and concentrated, so he can master his moves, almost in a state of meditation. Here and now, nothing else exists except the lacquer line. All his energy is concentrated on this instant and the line he's applying in one breath. He is the paintbrush, he is the bowl, he is the entire universe, and the complete universe is contained in this line and this single breath.

This is a beautiful metaphor for life, in that it's important to concentrate all your force and all your energy on one precise goal. You're never more efficient, than when your attention is completely turned toward a single objective, in this state of grace, this altered state of mind described as "flow" by positive psychology, when you are "in the zone." Every one of your moves and thoughts is being suspended in another time zone, with a precise slowness where time expands until it doesn't exist any longer.

Personally, I am "in the zone," feeling the flow, when I'm writing and when I practice the art of kintsugi. In my previous life, I would have been busy with too many things at the same time to savor this pleasure. I would have found it too slow and inefficient . . . Now I have daily proof of my progress. For instance, when speaking on the phone, I now prefer to concentrate completely on my conversation, so focused that I can even detect if the person on the other end of the line is doing something else while talking to me. Now I concentrate 100 percent on my current activity and enjoy the journey instead of trying to arrive before I've left . . . The art of kintsugi is a good teacher for patience and concentration!

Kintsugi, like other Japanese arts, teaches you how to focus your vital energy (chi) on one thing at a time. In today's world, with its many demands and temptations, you can easily disperse and dissolve your energy through stress, agitation, and vain distractions. Rediscover your center and your chi. What is your goal? Be rigorous and focus all of your effort toward achieving your objective instead of dispersing your energy by fluttering from one thing to the next.

Centered and concentrated in every one of your moves and intentions, visualize your goal; nothing else is more important.

Control your thoughts, your moves, your words, and your actions. Focus, aim, hold your breath . . . Shoot and let your arrow fly toward your target.

The Way

The art of *kyudo* is the art of traditional Japanese archery. The required posture and concentration train the practitioner to recognize the sensations of his body. He channels his breathing, learning to calm his mind and to control his emotions, aiming for victory, not over his adversary but over himself.

The *kyudo* (Way of the Bow) follows the same philosophy as all the other Ways. In Japanese *do* means "the Way," such as in:

- **Shodo**: Way of Calligraphy

- **Chado**: Way of Tea

- **Kendo**: Way of Sword

- **Judo**: Way of Suppleness

- **Aikido**: Way of Cooperating Energies

- **Kado**: Way of Flowers

All of these arts have three elements in common: mindfulness, alertness, and concentration. All of them are necessary to reach self-realization. When you are completely present, the sword, the bowl, the paintbrush becomes an extension of your arm, of your being, just as you, yourself, are an extension of the universe . . . In becoming "one" with your action, being present here and now, you take the first step "on the Way."

The Way is a long path toward finalizing your self-realization by expanding your mindfulness to realize your true nature and enlightenment: total emptiness and permanence of the mind, the moment you touch eternity . . . Isn't the art of Kintsugi a Way too? Kintsugi-do . . .

What About You?

Are you focused in what you are doing, or do you scatter and disperse your time? What if you concentrated all of your vital energy toward one unique goal, the one that's really important to you?

It's Time to Act!

The Target

The *kyudo* metaphor is here to help you concentrate your mind on one particular target with all your energy.

❶ Take some time alone. Make sure not to be disturbed during the next few minutes, and settle yourself comfortably. Concentrate on your target. What is it? What is hidden deep in your heart? What do you want to concentrate all of your vital energy, all of your chi, on?

❷ Write this goal on the center of this traditional *kyudo* target.

❸ Center yourself.

❹ Firmly entrench yourself.

❺ Concentrate all of your energy on your vital center, the Japanese *hara*, located on your belly, between your pubis and your belly button, corresponding to the second chakra (the sacred orange chakra, the zone of instinct and creative emotions).

❻ Mentally focus.

❼ Awaken your vigilance.

❽ Lift up your bow.

❾ Aim at your target.

❿ Sense how your body, your mind, your heart, your bow, your arrow, and your target become one, "the perfect union."

⓫ In *kyudo*, only the "true," "good," and "beautiful" gesture (*shin, zen, bi*) releases the arrow in the center of the target . . . Shoot the arrow: This is the moment of truth.

⓬ Follow the release of the arrow . . .

⓭ Visualize the arrow perfectly hitting the center.

⓮ Contemplate and self-reflect . . .

Go Further . . .

Look at some videos, or even better, arrange for an initiation to the Japanese art of *kyudo*.

Start Here and Now!

Write your goal on the center of the *kyudo* target.

Access the next level
of your life.

ADD

Hasten slowly, and without losing heart,
put your work twenty times upon the anvil.

—Nicolas Boileau

Polish the surface and apply a second fine layer of red lacquer (*e-urushi*, or *neri bengara-urushi*).

The art of kintsugi requires a great deal of patience. Layer upon layer, slowly but surely, the cure continues.

In all areas, in life too, several passes are often required to succeed.

Challenges to be tackled anew, recurrent patterns, learning based on repetition . . . Twenty times, sometimes one hundred, you need to resume the Work of your life as if it were the first time. To start again, time after time, can be long and slow, and sometimes outright discouraging. You may have the impression that you're not going forward but remaining at the same spot, without understanding Why! Actually, this is not completely lost time . . . it's called "mastering." Mastering of a practice, mastering of the mind. It's the acquisition of mastery of one move and one thought at one time.

And suddenly, one day it all becomes clear! Suddenly a new lesson has been learned. You have reached another level of learning, the connections are being made, it's an epiphany, the famous "eureka!" moment.

I love this moment when everything becomes clear and falls into place. Before, I was simply not ready to understand . . . For example, I enjoy reading books or watching movies over and over again, to enjoy a new aspect in every pass. By watching and rereading them, each time I reach a different level of the message, noticing a new sentence or a new scene, which gives me an entirely new understanding.

So you too should patiently continue your efforts, your progression layer upon layer, page by page, scene after scene, thought after thought, until you have reached this step when all becomes clear. Access the next level of your life.

The Art of *Fuki Urushi*

Japanese arts often proceed slowly and with great patience, layer upon layer, in order to bring out the full beauty of the object. As in kintsugi, *fuki urushi* uses the same *urushi* lacquer, but natural (translucent, without pigment, the same lacquer that is used by the kintsugi master to glue the broken pieces together). With Japanese lacquer art, often the colors red and black come to mind. Therefore you can't perceive the natural aspect of the wood hidden beneath successive layers of lacquer. The *fuki urushi* technique attempts to create the opposite effect, highlighting the beauty of the grain of the wood: The artist first applies a thin layer of lacquer to a well-prepared object, then immediately wipes it before placing the object in the *muro* to dry for one or two days. Then he sands it, only to repeat the procedure many times (up to eight layers).

This technique allows him to enhance the beauty of the object's natural surface, instead of hiding it, by "listening to the voice of wood." This is another way to look at things, searching for truth and authenticity.

What About You?

Are you impatient to see the end result? And what if, instead of being discouraged, you understood that each phase is a necessary progression and could wait patiently for a new level of understanding?

It's Time to Act!

The Next Level

Do you have a favorite movie or book? One that you've seen or read time and again, over time, maybe even since you were a child?

By loving it above all others, it's probable that it has a special message for you that strikes a chord internally. It speaks directly to your subconscious. Could it have a message to convey if you were to explore it one more time?

❶ Write down the name of the book or film you'd like to read or see again.

_____

❷ Without looking or reading it yet, write down all of the emotions it evokes.

_____

_____

_____

_____

❸ Now watch it or read it again with fresh eyes, in full appreciation of every scene. Try to really "taste" it, as if you were discovering it for the first time.

❹ How do you feel?

_____

_____

_____

_____

❺ What does it say about you?

_____

_____

_____

❻ What message does it convey today?

_____

_____

_____

_____

❼ Absorb it . . .

_____

_____

_____

_____

Go Further . . .

Watch a film or read a book that you loved above all others as a child or teenager but that you haven't seen or read again since. I remember that I once asked the best student in my preparatory MBA class what he did during his vacation. He confided in me that he read and reread every year . . . _Noddy_! Immerse yourself in an earlier time, rediscover your youth, travel through time, remember that delicious moment that speaks to you like the madeleine of Marcel Proust . . . What is it whispering to you?

Start Here and Now!

Select a book or movie you'd like to rediscover and place it in view next to your bed or on your coffee table.

Reanimate yourself!

REANIMATE

To live is the rarest thing in the world. Most people exist, that is all.

—Oscar Wilde

The joints are finally covered by beautiful red lacquer. Brilliant and free-flowing veins have cured the object to give it a second chance. Put it in the box for half an hour.

Patiently, the kintsugi master, week after week, layer upon layer, has gathered, bandaged, and cared for the object. Now he will reanimate it. Soon it will be revealed in all of its splendor.

Sometimes in life you forget one "little" detail: TO LIVE! You're satisfied to just survive, to just exist, going from point A to point B. Every day it's the same old routine: commute, work, television, sleep . . . Does this remind you of someone?

Personally, I've already been trying to fight this force of inertia for a long time. To start with I don't have a television. What an enormous time-saver! And I simply refuse to give in to the desire to become addicted to any kind of technology. When I went to New York to join my future husband, he had been living in the same mode for twenty years. He lived a few steps away from what most people only dream of, without taking advantage of it. (Any Parisian who has never visited the Louvre or Versailles might understand what I'm talking about.) So I decided to take control by creating an intensive "reanimation program" by discovering New York from the inside, the New York of real New Yorkers. No visit to the Statue of Liberty this time! In ten days we saw four interactive and immersive plays, tried flying trapeze, went to the beach, enjoyed vegetarian dishes at a three-star restaurant, contemplated cherry blossoms, wandered through Luna Park, took an aerial tram, enjoyed parasailing, crossed the Brooklyn Bridge, relaxed in a spa, bought an inspirational bottle of "intuition" from the official superhero supply store, launched wish boats on the Hudson River, teased fireflies and black squirrels, visited two museums, and undertook a pilgrimage to Princeton (in Einstein's footsteps). We had not seen each other for twenty years and wanted to celebrate our reunion. That certainly was a lively vacation, shaking us up in every sense of the word.

We all need lightness and fantasy in our lives. Look at the unexpected success of the movie *La La Land*. You too can transform your life into a musical comedy, where you are the author, actor, dancer, scriptwriter, producer, director, casting director, lighting technician, makeup artist, and hairdresser. It's up to you to choose the theme and the actors. But don't forget one detail: In the movie of your life, there are no dress rehearsals and there is just a single take!

Now then, don't you have anything better to do with your life than be half asleep? It's time to wake up! Take action now and rise! John Lennon said, "Life is what happens while you are busy making other plans." And without realizing it, life passes you by . . . Would you prefer a sparkling and explosive life, or the mediocre version? Do you prefer to live in HD (high definition) or in low definition? Breathe air into your life and rediscover what makes you live again.

Reanimate yourself!

The *Yes Man* Spirit

For inspiration I invite you to watch or watch again the Peyton Reed movie with Jim Carrey. The hero leads a life filled with depression, gloom, and repetitiveness. Almost like he's half-dead . . .

One day, by accident, he's participating in a personal-development seminar and is invited to say "Yes!" to life, according to a simple methodology: Never refuse an opportunity anymore. He therefore starts to say "yes" in any kind of occasion, and his life becomes radically transformed.

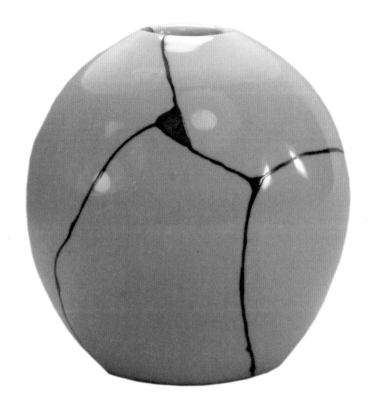

What About You?

Are you really alive? Are you saying "Yes!" to life, or are you holding yourself back using any possible excuse? What if you got out of your comfort zone in order to finally start to feel completely alive?

It's Time to Act!

The List of Your Life's Desires

I invite you to list all of your life's desires!

❶ To start with, in order to see more clearly, list everything that moves you and that you have accomplished already. All those moments that made you really feel alive, explode with joy, be in harmony with yourself.

❷ Read this list over again and search for common themes that are being regularly repeated: Sports? Relaxation? Adrenaline? Care? Exoticism? Music? Friends? Creativity? Children? Love? It's probably what touches you the most . . .

❸ The idea is to rediscover that vibration. How do these themes inspire you? Note a new desire with the same theme that you'd like to explore very soon, something you've always dreamed of doing, to put life back into your life.

❹ Make an appointment with yourself . . .

Life desires already accomplished	Theme(s)	Next life desires with the same theme(s)

Go Further . . .

Make a deal with yourself to accomplish one of your next life desires every month!

Start Here and Now!

In your diary, enter right now a first life desire to fulfill. And if possible, take the first step to get there: Inform all concerned persons and book the desired activity.

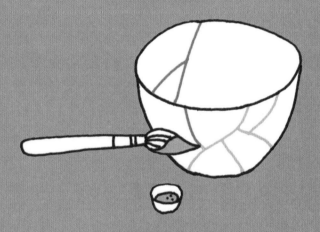

STAGE 5

REVEAL

落花枝に帰ると見れば胡蝶かな
rakka eda ni / kaeru to mireba / kochō kana

The falling flower
I saw drift back to the branch
was a butterfly.

Arakida Moritake
(1473–1549)

Live, love, laugh!

ILLUMINATE

. . . being firmly persuaded that every time a man smiles,—but much more so, when he laughs, it adds something to this Fragment of Life.

—Laurence Sterne

While the lacquer is still moist and sticky, delicately apply the gold powder to the lacquer with a brush or a metal application tool (without touching it, as it is still fresh).

After a long wait and much work, here is the long-anticipated final moment where you add the gold dust to the fresh lacquer along the cracked lines. Each particle of the gold powder will become one with the lacquer, giving the impression of gold flowing along the fissures.

Gold is a strong symbol, representing purity, perfection, value, and light . . . After all your phases of curing, cleaning, effort, and progress, you are now ready to sparkle. How long has it been since you treated yourself like a precious object? The time has come to illuminate your life . . . to add sparkles, smiles, and laughter, and maybe even a touch of silliness! Everything you might have forgotten over the years . . .

On a personal level, after all the challenges I have been through, I was still surrounded by a heavy cloud of sadness. I used to be a radiant little girl. But that was a long time ago . . . and now I found myself huddled in a corner because of all my sufferings. I had forgotten how to laugh, I even had forgotten how to smile.

Interestingly enough, I had started my personal exploration with laughing therapies: clown workshops, comedies, improv, and laughter yoga! And I had selected a therapist who specialized in connecting with your inner child.

Bit by bit, I heal my wounds and sprinkle them with gold, rediscovering my former lightness and sparkle, putting laughter back into my daily life. As the saying goes, once the student is ready, the master appears. Isn't that perfect? I had a second master right at home in my own daughter. She is a real little laughing Buddha, a true force of cheerfulness and magic. Her bursts of laughter slowly soothe my frozen heart, melting the protective layers with a whirlwind of living, adding lightness in our daily lives. She puts me back on my path.

What if you too were to take everything not so seriously? Add some glitter and gold to your life, a bit of silliness, one touch of tickles, a dose of joy. Smile, laugh and giggle, make faces, jump on a trampoline, sparkle, and connect with your inner child! Turn the bursts in your life into bursts of laughter. Live, love, laugh!

The Laughing Buddha

Westerners often confuse the Buddha Siddhārtha Gautama with the smiling Buddha of good life, who is often represented sitting with a contagious smile on his face or standing with two raised arms. In Japanese mythology, he is one of the seven gods (kamis) of Fortune and represents abundance, good health, contentment, and commerce.

In Japan he represents the itinerant monk Hotei (Budai or Pu-Tai in China), who lived during the tenth century. He was an eccentric Zen master, jovial, benevolent, and generous, who wandered from village to village to accomplish his mission. Legend has it that he put broken wooden toys in his bag and returned them repaired with sweets for the children. Once he was done with distributing toys and sweets, he looked at the sky, raised his arms, and burst out laughing in such a contagious way that the entire village started laughing with him. At that point, he could leave to accomplish his mission of spreading joy and happiness elsewhere!

When he was asked why he acted the way he did, he answered that his bag contained life's heavy burdens, and it was best to put it on the ground to lighten the load. Legend has it that he was such a joker that he made people laugh even after his death: He asked to be cremated (which was not the Buddhist practice at the time), and during his cremation fireworks suddenly illuminated the sky. He had hidden firecrackers in his clothing . . .

Tradition says that rubbing the tummy on one of his many statues results in instant happiness. When you too are in a sullen or morose mood, connect to the energy of this jolly Buddha!

Laughter Yoga

When we are relaxed and happy, smiling and laughing is easy. But, paradoxically, even when we force a fake smile or laughter, we are sending a message to the brain that we are happy, making it believe that we are. We therefore have the ability to actually make ourselves happy! Our brain and our body do not differentiate between a fake laugh and a natural one. The brain's endorphins are released, and the physiological benefits (stimulating and analgesic) are the same: They are natural opiates, creating effects similar to those of morphine! Not to mention that laughing is also beneficial for the abs . . .

It's according to those principles that laughter yoga was invented in India during the 1990s. The founder, Dr. Madan Kataria, summarizes it perfectly like this: "I am not laughing because I am happy, I am happy because I am laughing." Since then, laughter yoga clubs have spread across the planet.

Don't panic if you're not flexible. Laughing yoga is not based on physical postures but rather on a certain lightness of spirit, on not taking oneself too seriously. It's therefore accessible to all ages (I have taken my daughter to sessions since she was three years old), and different physical conditions, even though one has to move at least a little. (Although it is not advised during pregnancy because of diaphragm contractions.) For one hour, you let yourself go and connect with your inner child.

A typical session starts with a warm-up period of stimulating laughter: *ho, ho, ha, ha, ha,* while clapping your hands. And then, depending on each particular session, perhaps a few silly exercises to mobilize the body, to fully contract the diaphragm, to liberate the endorphins, and to stimulate laughter through dancing, singing, and improv. A session might consist of imitating a chicken, presenting yourself to a crowd as a celebrity star, dancing like you're possessed, imitating a cross-country skier, or pretending to dry the paint on your fingernails. You always use your diaphragm when breathing to simulate the contractions of laughter. This provides a warm-up for the grand and contagious final session, when all the participants laugh together, with continuous explosions of laughter. The forced laughter at the beginning is simulated but becomes spontaneous and self-propagating by the end.

The best way to understand is to test it!

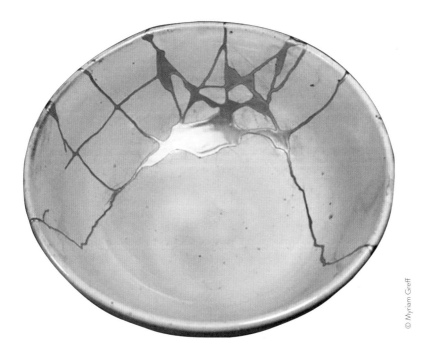

What About You?

Do you manage to find lightness and joy in your daily life, or are you overwhelmed by your injuries? What if you tried a laughter and silliness therapy, to reconnect to your inner child, and heal your wounds with glitter and gold?

It's Time to Act!

The Reconnection with Your Inner Child

This visualization helps you find the emotions hidden within your inner child and to listen to what he/she is whispering to liberate you.

❶ Settle into your ideal position: Get comfortable, quiet, calm, alone, and have some crayons and something to write on within reach.

❷ Take thirty deep and slow breaths to relax. Take your time.

❸ Contact the inner child within you. Gently approach him/her and let your inner child manifest slowly. Where is he/she hidden? In your stomach, your solar plexus, your throat, or your heart? There aren't any wrong answers. Feel his/her arrival and observe your sensations.

❹ Focus on your search: Do you see him/her? Is your inner child a boy or a girl? (Sometimes we visualize a child of the opposite sex.) What does he/she look like? What is he/she wearing?

❺ Let your inner child approach at his/her own pace . . .

❻ Connect with your inner child and observe your own feelings: What is his/her personality? Is your inner child shy, forceful, exuberant, calm, furious, stressed out, or happy?

❼ Look, your inner child has brought you a present. What is it that he/she brought you? Can you visualize it? A big bag, a treasure chest, in his/her hands, in his/her pockets or backpack . . .

❽ Open the present. What does it contain?

❾ Give your inner child a big hug and thank him/her from the bottom of your heart.

⑩ Cuddle with him/her.

⑪ Listen, your inner child has something to tell you before leaving. He/she whispers something in your ear . . .

⑫ Invite him/her to come back as often as he/she wants to.

⑬ Tell your inner child goodbye and let him/her leave.

⑭ Concentrate on your emotions. How do you feel?

⑮ Immediately write down this visualization, describing it with words and images, noting all your sensations.

⑯ Infuse the feeling . . .

Go Further . . .

Revive the experience by engaging in an activity you loved as a child, whether it's coloring, shaping Silly Putty, jumping on a trampoline, or watching a cartoon you loved, to get back in touch with the emotions of your childhood.

Start Here and Now!

Listen to music from your childhood (ideally a song from the cartoon you watched) that transports you instantly back to that time.

**Treasure the gold
of your life.**

COLLECT

The future is nothing but organizing the present. Your task is not to foresee it, but to enable it.

—Antoine de Saint-Exupéry

Save any remaining gold powder for your next creation. Then put the object back into the box for two to three days for drying and hardening.

Gold is very precious . . . and very valuable: Kintsugi is an expensive craft if one follows the proper process and uses real gold! It would be a shame to lose even a single milligram . . . Therefore the challenge is to recover the maximum amount of gold powder after its dispersal from the object, as well as from the work surface, to keep all one can for the next creation.

Sometimes in life it may also be necessary to collect our memories in order to take stock of every little ounce of happiness. There are two ways of doing this: First and foremost, by living every moment in a state of complete mindfulness and awareness to experience it to its fullest potential. This is the "live streaming," in four dimensions and HD! Secondly, by noting it down somehow to preserve a trace of it, like a treasure. This is the "replay," transmitting wonder and gratitude. All the positive psychology studies agree on this point: Being mindful of our everyday luck, we automatically increase our well-being.

This exercise can take various written or oral forms: a gratitude book, album of memories, diary, smartphone application, video, blog, social networking, letter or e-mail addressed to your "future self," souvenir chest, scrapbook, thank-you prayer, computer listing . . . it's for you to decide what suits you best!

Personally, I've kept a "positive journal" for the last ten years in which I note everything that I do each day, but always with a positive insight on things. It's essential to carefully word one's thoughts, because the brain registers the main message without paying too much attention to "details," such as negative wording. So for instance if you write, "I didn't have an accident," your brain has the tendency to only retain the word "accident."

I attach a photo taken of my family on January 1 to the cover of my positive journal. On the first few pages, I write down my mantra of the moment and my projects for the year, so I can evaluate my annual progress. Every single day, I write down all the positive things that happened—whether big or small joys. This may range from "taking a bath by candlelight" to "getting acquainted with my daughter" on the day I gave birth to her! This is a very interesting exercise, because given a certain amount of time, it programs our brain to perceive what happens around us as positive (the famous "glass half full"), allowing us to tackle our challenges with greater ease. In this manner, even when my world collapsed around me on the day I learned that I was getting divorced, I found the strength to write positive entries in my journal, and only positive ones. The brain is like a muscle you train: Adding strength to one's positive thoughts, lifting them up to be more joyful, is preferable to giving in to lower vibrations.

This is also a great way to gather your memories, so you can revisit them with pleasure when needed. I do the same daily exercise for my two daughters, noting every day in their personalized positive journals their joys, their first times, and their progress since the day they were born. It's a good way to share and communicate with them until someday they write their own positive journal.

You too like a squirrel preparing for winter can collect a good reserve of memories, gather bursts of laughter, and store some seeds of joy! You can enjoy these when you feel blue. Treasure the gold of your life!

The Symbolism of Gold

Kintsugi can be practiced using any kind of metal: gold, silver, copper, or brass . . . But it's gold that's universally acclaimed. It has a symbolic value established for thousands of years and is venerated by almost all civilizations as the most precious metal and as a general measure of exchange.

Its physical qualities are important: It is unalterable, hypoallergenic, and an excellent thermal and electrical conductor. Furthermore, it is easy to transform or polish, whether into threads as thin as hair or into a thin sheet (1/10,000 of a millimeter) that is almost translucent.

But its aura goes well beyond its physical properties. Gold is as luminous as a burst of sunlight . . . With its cosmic origin, it is sacred and worshipped, representing total knowledge, purity, spirituality, and perfection. These symbols and messages are found in a lot of examples. For instance, consider the symbolism of the gold medal, regarded as the highest reward in sport; the golden age, which represents the height of a civilization; the golden crown of a king, which is supposed to channel divine energy; the mythological golden apple, object of all desire . . . And also gold is featured in the golden halos of saint icons, the golden ring of fairy tales and unions, the golden sickle of the druids to cut the holy mistletoe, the Golden Fleece, the golden eggs laid by a magical goose, the alchemy experiments, the golden Buddha statues . . .

What About You?

Do you live every moment in HD, streaming live? What if you lived in total awareness, treasuring each moment and each souvenir as gold in your life?

It's Time to Act!

The Treasures of Your Life

Plan ahead and create for yourself a survival kit! One day when you feel particularly good and full of energy, collect together all of your best souvenirs and all the best things you've done. Put them in order to create a real "treasure chest." For example it might include the following:

- A list of your favorite music
- A DVD of your best "feel-good" movie
- A sample of a perfume that inspires joyful memories
- A soft blanket
- A delicious snack
- A perfumed tea bag
- A movie ticket to give yourself a moment of relaxation
- A list of great addresses to escape to
- A toy from your childhood
- A book you adore
- A recipe for your favorite meal
- A snow globe
- A decorative object you love
- A comic book that makes you laugh
- A picture that moves you
- A reproduction of your favorite painting
- A photo album of good memories

- A lucky charm

- A list of stimulating activities

- A list of compliments

- A beautiful letter that you write to yourself

- A beautiful letter you received some time ago

- Bath salts or oils

- Glitter and confetti

- Beautiful postcards with positive messages

- A notebook for writing and drawing

- A lovely poem or haiku

- A security blanket . . .

Put together all the things that make you feel good and appeal to all five of your senses. After all, who knows you better than yourself? This will be a "lucky dip," preciously guarded to open only in case of emergencies . . .

Go Further . . .

Thanksgiving is not just about eating turkey and pumpkin pie! But it's about everyone expressing individually those things in their lives that they are most grateful for. What if you were to introduce this little ritual to your family for everyone to express his or her gratitude on a daily basis?

Start Here and Now!

Choose your first memory and put it in your treasure chest!

Reveal yourself!

EMERGE

*It is by believing in roses
that you make them bloom.*

—Anatole France

Once the lacquer has dried, use a silk cotton ball to gently remove any excess gold powder.

Finally, the key moment. The time has come for the object to emerge fully cured and magnificent, revealing itself in all its splendor. Its life lines are now sublimated with gold. This process has provided the opportunity for transformation. The object has healed, transmuted its injuries, and re-created itself. Even more beautiful, more unique, more precious for having been injured . . .

I too have the feeling that I am about to emerge and bloom. I feel that I am on the right path, because lately my friends and family have told me that I seem younger than before. It's like I have been liberated from a heavy load, as if I have eliminated a layer of anger, a layer of sadness, a layer of fear, a layer of stress, a layer of denial, and have finally emerged. I do have emotional scars, but I am more alive than ever before, with a smooth forehead and more relaxed features. Peace and quiet after the storm . . . Even my wrinkles are less noticeable! I often surprise myself with a smile on my lips, even in the middle of a traffic jam.

For you too, this may well be the time to bloom. You have taken all this time and all this energy to get over your injuries, you took care of yourself like a precious object deserving all the gold of this world. It's the moment to be reborn and reveal yourself!

From Lip Balm to Heart Balm

The socio-aesthetic therapy helps those people having the greatest need to reveal themselves.

This discipline appears to be superficial, but in fact it deeply touches the soul: With makeup, personal care, and being well-dressed, such people will finally rediscover their self-esteem. Finally, they are no longer invisible. Finally, they can look at themselves in the mirror, because they are worth it.

Consider for instance a famous Los Angeles hairdresser who usually charges thousands of dollars for every haircut but who also offers homeless people makeovers free of charge: By doing so, he gives them faith in life and new confidence. Or those beauticians who give people in prison some of their humanity back by simply offering to care for them. Or those associations that provide new outfits to job seekers for interviews: It goes way beyond just a new look. Or those beauticians who go to retirement homes to offer makeup and hair styling to elderly people, giving them the desire to smile again. Or those practitioners offering massages and aesthetic care to hospitalized people to assist them in accepting their new bodies, sometimes transformed by their illnesses or injuries . . .

It's a noble discipline: It supports and accompanies people during their difficult challenges and their metamorphoses.

What About You?

After all your ordeals, do you feel that the moment has come to reveal yourself in all of your splendor, to be reborn?

It's Time to Act!

The Fresh Start

This stage needs to be highlighted and celebrated! When you feel that the moment has come, I invite you to enjoy your fresh start with a personal ceremony. Celebrate yourself, you are so worth it!

Some people mark the occasion with their family and friends, for instance when they get divorced. Here I suggest you make this a more personal and private celebration.

Clean up and tidy your home, prepare yourself a delicious meal, buy yourself some flowers, wear a beautiful outfit, choose some inspiring music, put some perfume or cologne on yourself as if you were going on a special date. And in fact that is what you are doing here: having a meeting with your new self!

Close your eyes and visualize your rebirth. Imagine that you are a butterfly on the verge of its metamorphosis, coming out of its chrysalis. That cocoon you are leaving behind represents all of your ordeals, all of your injuries, whether they are emotional or physical. You have consciously decided to leave all of your suffering behind. Look at that shapeless pile. It is now in the past. You're out of here. For the first time, you see the light; for the first time, you see clearly.

Gently and cautiously, try out your golden wings. Let them flutter in the wind. Spread them out in the sun so they can catch a ray of sunshine and sparkle. Take off, flying toward your new life . . .

Savor this new sensation for several minutes until it becomes well-grounded inside you.

Then taste that delicious meal you prepared for yourself.

Go Further . . .

To remember the moment, add a souvenir to this ceremony: a gift to yourself, a new outfit, a new object, a piece of music, a new perfume. It will become the symbol of your new departure. For example, after each divorce, I sold my wedding ring and offered myself a significant present to remind myself of my strengths and my survival: an indirect gesture to transform my gold into healing, in the kintsugi spirit.

Start Here and Now!

Arrange for a date with yourself by writing down the day and time of your fresh start ceremony.

Never ever again accept the unacceptable.

PROTECT

Pain is inevitable.
Suffering is optional.
—Haruki Murakami

To protect the golden joints, apply a fine layer of protective lacquer. After five minutes, gently dab the joints. Then let the object dry for twenty-four hours.

The gold should be covered by a thin layer of lacquer so it can be protected and preserve its glow. Even after the last stage has been finalized, one needs to treat the object with care: It's recommended not to use the object for several months in order to protect its fresh repair. Consider the object to be still convalescent; the lacquer is a living product and will continue to harden, like bones tend to consolidate after having been set. In this manner the object reinforces its newfound strength over time.

Like in the art of Kintsugi, you too should protect yourself. You were just reborn. Your injuries just finished healing. It's important not to open them imprudently. In order to avoid a relapse, avoid harmful influences, negative judgments, bad vibes, or general pessimism.

For example, why should you suffer daily depressing news? Or listen to a friend on the phone complaining for hours without taking any interest in you? Or attend a family dinner during which your life choices will be dissected and criticized?

Don't agree to an invitation from people you don't particularly care for. Don't fill your agenda with too many obligations. Don't feel obliged when nothing or nobody can force you . . . it's the fastest way to a relapse.

Some people, without even realizing it, literally put negative pressure on you. Like "energy vampires," they feed from your good vibes, your smile, and your goodwill. The better you feel, the more they resent it. With small and disagreeable remarks, scathing wit, "innocent" small quips, passive-aggressive remarks, or emotional blackmail, they can leave you lifeless, exhausted, bled dry, with a heavy guilt feeling, without even understanding what just happened. They might say things like: "Oh, you are always so lucky!" "After everything I have done for you . . ." "If you do that, I won't love you anymore." "You have no idea what just happened to me again . . ." Sometimes just their presence, filled with the negative emotions of past events, may drain all your energy! Like content leeches, they let go to return to their own lives, but at your expense. Beware, sometimes one can even be an energy vampire without even realizing it. For example, it was mostly my mother who was "vampirizing" me. After spending time with her, I was always completely exhausted, even when everything went well between us. It took me three days to recover from family celebrations! Imagine how I was feeling when I moved into the apartment across the hall. A true example of badly cut apron strings!

Having just overcome your injuries, it's essential that you protect yourself against anything that might get you down, such as negative people draining your energy, malignant narcissists, generalized depression, psychological attacks, depressing information, false duties, gloom, ugliness, mediocrity, and general pettiness . . .

Create a protective wellness cocoon around yourself. Surround yourself with caring and happy people, beautiful objects, soft blankets, soothing music, and bright colors. Fill your day with smiles and laughter, good news, positive vibes, the beauty of nature . . .

Have the courage to break free and to say "No" to protect your glow or preserve yourself. Never ever again accept the unacceptable.

© Céline Santini

189

The Seven Kamis of Fortune

Japanese Shinto ("divine path") is not a religion but rather a spiritual practice in search of harmony, truth, and peace, through which one connects with the divine aspect of nature's purity and universality. This kind of animism personifies nature's energy, as well as ancestors, or ancestral mythology, in the form of spirits: the kamis.

To translate *kami* as "god" is somewhat simplistic and may confuse Westerners. It is more of an energy or a spirit. Japanese tradition has an incalculable number of kamis. There may be as many as eight million, a number that symbolizes infinity. You're perhaps already familiar with a famous kami called Totoro!

Among the most popular kamis are the seven kamis of fortune (*shichi fukujin*), one woman and six men:

- **Benzaiten,** kami of arts, eloquence, wisdom, science, and beauty
- **Bishamonten,** kami of war and prosperity
- **Daikokuten,** kami of wealth, household, and kitchen
- **Ebisu,** kami of fishermen, merchants, honest work, and prosperity
- **Fukurokuju,** kami of longevity, wealth, fertility, virility, and wisdom
- **Hotei,** kami of abundance, good health, contentment, and commerce
- **Jurojin,** kami of longevity and prosperity

It's believed that these seven kamis of fortune arrive on Earth each December 31 in their boat to distribute happiness, luck, and gifts to good people. That evening Japanese children put a symbol of the kamis' boat under their pillows, in order to benefit from their protection throughout the year.

What About You?

Do you know how to say NO? Do you know how to protect yourself against bad vibes or people who drain your energy? What if you learned how to protect yourself in order to maintain your balance and your vibrancy?

It's Time to Act!

The Altar for Protection

In their homes, Japanese Shinto believers set up a small altar for protection, called *kamidana* ("spirit shelf"). It's a place to put ancestors' pictures, candles, offerings . . . It also has a removable shutter for hiding objects representing secret wishes, like photographs and other things. Whatever your beliefs may be, you can create a personal, small altar for protection in the same spirit.

Go Further . . .

To protect yourself against bad vibes, meditate and visualize a protective cocoon of vibrant, luminous energy around you.

Start Here and Now!

Imagine and create your own protection ritual.

Nurture your uniqueness!

PERSONALIZE

The part in each of us that we feel is different from other people is just the part that is rare, the part that makes our special value—and that is the very thing people try to suppress.

—André Gide

Use a tool you like to work with and that appeals to you to polish the golden joints. Some kintsugi masters use agate stones; others use ivory, fish teeth, or hematite stones.

Each master approaches the art of kintsugi in his unique manner, by carefully selecting his tools, the chest in which he organizes his materials, or the box that contains the precious gold powder. The choice of the polishing utensil used to give the gold its splendor is especially symbolic. It's the last tool to be used during the final stage of the metamorphosis. It's therefore necessary to appropriately select a utensil of personal preference, without necessarily following what others might have chosen before.

In life as well, it may be necessary to walk your own way and to nurture your uniqueness and distinctiveness. Are you different? Good for you! Personally, I don't hesitate to open new paths. My only compass is my gut feeling. If I feel good about it, I go for it, without being concerned what others might think! Incidentally, I do love vintage things, unique pieces, handmade projects, and transforming every single object into something special. It's all part of a global spirit: career

(I always follow my gut feeling, particularly if it appears to be impossible!); attitude (I can't go with the crowd when I find the situation absurd); clothing (I find it perfectly okay to pair a bright-red coat with a fuchsia scarf and an orange sweater, or wear a hat in the shape of a strawberry); decoration (yes, I live in *Alice in Wonderland* decor); entertainment (my famous dinners in the dark); and all the little details of my life (I always personalize all the gifts I receive). The ultimate stage certainly is the art of kintsugi: I delight in repairing each object with the greatest of care, transforming it into something more precious and unique.

Do you really want to fit in with the crowd and live like a shy chameleon who blends in? It may be time to accept and release your inner pink flamingo or vibrant roaring lion!

Choose a distinctive sign, accept your differences and your eccentricities, stand out, free yourself, and nurture your uniqueness!

The Tattoo Therapy

Breast cancer is one of the most difficult ordeals to live through. It impacts women on several levels, certainly physically but also attacking their femininity and intimacy. Unfortunately, the scars from a mastectomy are quite visible, a daily reminder of past physical and psychological pain.

A new tendency is emerging to transcend the scar with therapeutic tattooing. The scar is covered with an artistic tattoo of significance to the woman being tattooed. It speaks of healing, resurrection, and resilience. It is there to express the force of life. Such a tattoo has more than aesthetic value: It completes the healing process. Carried on the chest like a warrior's medal, it symbolizes the victory of life, the return to beauty and sensuality, and emphasizes the unique path of each woman.

What About You?

Do you sometimes act like a chameleon to fit in with the crowd? And what if today you accepted and nurtured your uniqueness and distinctiveness?

It's Time to Act!

Ornamental Tattooing

Choose a sentence with special meaning to yourself, a phrase that symbolizes your healing. This is truly personal, but here are some examples: "What doesn't kill you makes you stronger," "This too shall pass," "Perfectly imperfect," "This is the first day of the rest of my life," "May you be happy," etc.

"Tattoo" this phrase somewhere in your home. You can write it on the wall using a marker, display it on a beautiful poster, save it as your screensaver, or have a giant sticker printed with this phrase, and so on.

Let it infuse your daily life so that you can soak in its energy and strength.

Go Further . . .

Tattoo that sentence onto your skin (with henna, or a more lasting option if you dare).

Start Here and Now!

Choose your phrase. What spontaneously comes to your mind?

_____

_____

_____

_____

_____

Glow with glory!

DAZZLE

Sublimity is the echo of greatness of spirit.

—Longinus

To make the gold shine, polish the object with a blend of oil and powder using the polishing tool you have selected.

Here is the final step of the long procedure. It requires making the gold shine by "waxing" it with a blend of oil and powder, and then burnishing it to make it sparkle.

You too are now reaching the final phase of your healing. Afterward all you will have to do is contemplate! It's time to shine and sparkle . . . Time to live, at last.

Finally you discover yourself with your particularities, your uniqueness, and your flaws fully accepted. You have worked hard and made daily progress, polishing your inner self layer after layer . . . Now the time has come to show your true nature and to diffuse your vibrancy and your light to the world!

Many things are not only physiological but also psychological. Think of great actors who manage to transform their energy by internalizing the personality they are representing!

To love oneself is not only a physical process, but most of all it's a state of mind. An anorexic person, unfortunately, will never find herself skinny enough, in full denial of reality.

I truly experienced the internal connection between body and mind the day I participated in a personal-development workshop while visiting the Royal Château de Blois in the Loire Valley. In a great hall, one could sit on a replica of a throne. Most of the visitors amused themselves by having their picture taken sitting on the royal seat. The speaker of the seminar used this opportunity for a little exercise: "Sit down on the throne like the queen or king you are." Everybody took their turn to try. It was very interesting to observe the subtle but clearly noticeable change in every person, like a special glow that suddenly changed every face. When it was my turn to sit on the throne, I connected with my inner queen. Spontaneously, I straightened my back, and I felt complete, serene, and strong. After the exercise, one of the participants said to me, "Before climbing on the throne you looked like a little girl. Once on the throne you changed into a woman."

Glowing therefore appears to be a choice. Like a living kintsugi, change the way you look upon yourself and assume your inner light and beauty. Take a few moments to observe the passage of time: that scar, that redness, those white hairs, that birthmark that makes you totally human. I know this subject well—I still have a cockeyed look despite all the years of treatment to correct my squint-eyed misalignment.

Be tolerant and forgiving of yourself, accept your imperfections, turn away from your complexes, concentrate on other parts of your body, or simply accept them. After all, they are part of you, make you special, and may even give you all your appeal! For example, after having tried every possible hair color to hide my white hairs, I now accept it by coloring my hair with a gold henna tone. In this manner golden threads enliven my dark hair, in a true kintsugi spirit!

A key moment arrives when your external appearance reflects your internal progress. Show your brilliance, stand up straight, diffuse your aura, assume the strength and splendor of the king or queen you are, and glow with glory!

The Flaws That Make You Unique

Paradoxically, your greatest strengths may reside within your perceived flaws, because they allow you to be different, if you accept them. Thanks to them, you are more unique and inimitable.

Would David Bowie have been David Bowie without his peculiar eyes? In show business, there are many successful stars with specific distinctiveness. Think of Meghan Trainor, who accepted her plump body; Winnie Harlow, the model who succeeded in spite of her skin problems; Jamel Debbouze, who did not let his handicap slow him down: "I see myself beautiful on a white horse. One does not need to see one's fate as a fatality. My accident has increased my strength tenfold." Lauren Wasser, the model with amputated legs: "Before, when everything was based on my physical appearance, I was an 'it' girl. Today I find myself more beautiful, inside and out." Rossy De Palma, a unique beauty in Picasso style: "One can't tell whether I am beautifully ugly or an ugly beauty." Sarah Jessica Parker, with her large nose. Christopher Lambert or Dalida with misaligned eyes. They all had beautiful careers by accepting their flaws. And they even used their physical flaws to emphasize their uniqueness!

So, rather than hiding your perceived flaws, what if you changed your strategy by giving them special value, like a living kintsugi?

What About You?

Do you feel dull or sparkling? What if you were finally proud of yourself and truly accepted yourself? Are you ready to glow and dazzle the world?

It's Time to Act!

The Inner Majesty

It's time to sit up straight, to accept your brilliance and your majesty. Have you ever noticed how many people on the street walk around bent over? Or the exact opposite, how a person full of presence and charisma usually holds his head upright? Your parents always said, "Stand up straight!" Perhaps they were right after all!

You too can reeducate yourself and find your inner queen or king. Stand up straight, holding your head as if you were wearing a golden crown. Imagine that your inner brightness also permeates your exterior, as if light rays emanate from you. In a nutshell, develop your aura. It's not easy at first, but it may quickly become automatic. Soon you'll not be able to do without it, and you won't even be able to see yourself with your head hanging down again. Your body will have registered the information in all of its cells!

Go Further . . .

Every morning, take advantage of every daily care task to implement a radiance ritual. Imagine that every drop of water or your shower gel transforms itself into light that enters your body. Rather than mechanically putting lotion on your body and face, do it mindfully. By touching your skin with your hands, imagine that gold and light permeate your insides all day long. Burnish yourself, radiate brilliance and vibrancy . . . Then straighten yourself up, look at yourself with a loving smile, even laugh at your reflection. Look, you are so dazzling!

Start Here and Now!

Visualize the cream or oil you use every day and, with your thoughts, fill it with light.

SUBLIMATE

梅が香にのつと日の出る山路哉

ume ga ka ni / notto hi no deru / yamaji kana

———

In the plum's fragrance
suddenly the sun—
mountain path.

Matsuo Bashō
(1644–1694)

**This is the first day
of the rest of your life.**

OBSERVE

And once the storm is over, you won't remember how you made it through, how you managed to survive. You won't even be sure whether the storm is really over. But one thing is certain. When you come out of the storm, you won't be the same person who walked in. That's what this storm's all about.

—Haruki Murakami

Take a step back and contemplate the repaired and sublimated object in all its uniqueness, strengthened by its veins of gold.

Like the object transformed by the art of kintsugi, revealing all of its splendor, as a phoenix rising from the ashes, you realize that you have been cured and transformed. You are ready!

The jigsaw puzzle has been assembled, the missing pieces have been replaced, the wounds have been treated and changed into scars covered in gold. Step back and connect with yourself, feeling how your new unity penetrates all of your cells. Experience this new sensation of being reborn, having survived. You are not in a thousand pieces anymore.

To reflect upon your revival, silence and solitude are necessary. Even the greatest men know how to regularly seek solitude: It's rumored that even Bill Gates limits his access to the screen, regularly enjoying lakeside digital detox!

I've noticed that, during key moments, it's important to be alone to face your fears and find yourself without trying to hide behind any kind of screen . . . or smoke screen. When I need a retreat, most of the time I simply stay at home. I take a real break for several days without any electronic connection. It's the best way to sit back and observe. Little by little, my real self emerges . . .

The injuries you've suffered in life present you with a second chance. Feel how the challenges you have overcome have made you a different person. Now you are actually yourself! This is the first day of the rest of your life.

The Tale of the Pot with a Crack

Legend has it that an old lady in China went to get water at a spring each day with two pots, each attached to the end of a pole. One of the pots was whole and the other had cracked. It was a long way from home to the spring. The whole pot was still full when the old lady had returned. But due to its crack, the other pot had lost water all the way home and arrived only half full.

The whole pot was very proud of its work. The cracked pot, on the other hand, felt belittled and useless. It was ashamed and sad to have accomplished only half of its task.

For two years, the old lady brought only one and a half pots of water home each day. Feeling like a failure, and not being able to take it any longer, the cracked pot addressed her, saying, "I'm ashamed of myself because I lose precious water every day."

The old lady smiled and answered, "Take a look at our path. Do you see the flowers on one side of the road but not on the other? It's on your side that the flowers have grown due to the water you've dropped every day. I have always known that you had a crack, and that's the reason I dropped flower seeds on your side of the path, so they could germinate and bloom. As a matter of fact, you have been watering them day after day. I thank you for all the beautiful flowers that brighten up my house every day due to your crack . . ."

What About You?

Can you see all the flowers you've brought into bloom along your thorny way?

It's Time to Act!

The Retreat

This is the time to step back and reflect, to accept the new person you are and to let go of the person you were. It's therefore the ideal moment to retreat and recognize your new self without filters, masks, or pretenses, without screens . . . or smoke screens.

According to your own aspirations, you can undertake a pilgrimage or a silent retreat, choose a mindfulness meditation center, a monastery, a cabin, a wooden hut, or simply stay at home. Do not forget to inform friends and family, because a real break can only be viable without Internet, television, or phone . . .

Then you can focus and meditate on your life's path, measure your progress on the route already covered, and lay the foundations for your new life.

Go Further . . .

Set up an annual date with yourself, as an irrevocable commitment.

Start Here and Now!

Save the date now for a one-on-one meeting with yourself!

You are a precious and invaluable jewel.

ADMIRE

Be yourself. Everyone else is already taken.

—Oscar Wilde

Notice how the broken object has been reborn and has become a precious work of art, unique and invaluable.

Life's accidents have created the fault lines of the broken object. As a result of the art of kintsugi, the object has experienced a metamorphosis. Its golden scars not only make it precious and original but inimitable as well.

As much as a kintsugi is one of a kind, have you fully realized how unique in the world you really are too? Nobody before you has ever lived exactly like you, with the same intensity, the same combination of experiences, with the same parents, friends, travels, ordeals, gifts, jobs, activities, hobbies, studies, losses, births, encounters . . . and nobody else can ever reproduce your path. The sum of your experiences, whether they have been pleasant or painful, have defined the person you are today.

For example, my own professional experience has certainly been atypical, with varying jobs lasting two months, one year, or ten years, including: project manager in a design agency, fragrance development manager, writer, art therapist, wedding planner, blogger, olfactory model, marketing professor, event teacher, online merchant, assistant nurse, telephone operator, personal-development coach, call center surveyor, creativity coach, human guinea pig, product manager, marketing study supervisor, and ceremony celebrant.

For a long time I worried about this apparently rambling path without a clear goal. Today I accept and cherish it . . . Each experience has helped me build myself. I have multipotentiality.

You too had a unique path in this world that contributed to defining who you are. Change your outlook: Accept your originality and your complexity. You are a precious and invaluable jewel.

Sculpture and Accidents

Sculpture is a field in which accidents are sometimes inevitable. A wrong stroke with the chisel, an unexpected shock, a slip of a tool, and it's a disaster: Everything has to be redone! How many masterpieces have thus disappeared? The artist has to work with the hidden veins in the stone, its softness or its hardness.

Rodin, known as the father of modern sculpture, enjoyed playing with these difficulties. He regularly welcomed and included accidents into his sculptures, looking for them to occur as part of the process of his creations.

To one of his students who broke a sculpture he said, "Dry your tears, my dear, and let me show you that what remains is perfectly sufficient to show your intention. You have to learn from your own accidents and silently transform them."

Was Rodin possibly a kintsugi master without even realizing it?

What About You?

Do you realize how unique and one of a kind you are, as a living kintsugi?

It's Time to Act!

The Life Line

Be mindful of your unique path and discover your life line.

❶ Take a white sheet of paper. Draw a horizontal line at the bottom of the page to represent your life, year after year.

❷ Don't forget to leave space for future years!

❸ On another sheet, list all the remarkable events in your life. These are the major milestones of your life line, the moments when your life crumbled or improved.

❹ Particularly note the most recent ordeals you have lived through.

❺ Organize them in chronological order.

❻ For each event, note the impact on your life and how you felt ("perception"), ranging from 1 to 10.

❼ Take the first sheet and plot each event as if it were on a graph. Connect the dots and observe the design of the line.

❽ Some periods are calm and neutral, where the line is quite horizontal. Other events are very intense and reflected in inflection points.

❾ Around each inflection point, note the main characters of your story.

❿ Sit back and analyze your path, discovering it for the first time.

⓫ Feel how unique in the world your path is, strengthening you from fault lines to lines of force.

Here is an example:

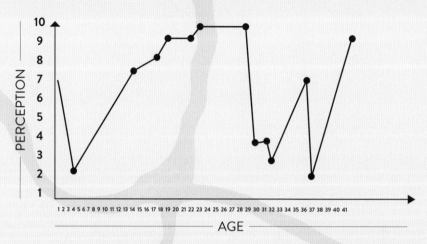

Go Further . . .

And if you're not completely convinced yet, ask friends and family members this simple question: "What do you think makes me unique in the world?"

Start Here and Now!

Take a sheet of paper and start drawing the horizontal line representing your life!

Continuously conjugate
your life from past tense to
present and future perfect!

CONTEMPLATE

*Only through suffering
can we find ourselves.*

—Fyodor Dostoyevsky

Remember the story behind the scars of the object.

Kintsugi accepts its injuries without hiding them. Covered with gold, they are glorified witnesses to the past and the shock experienced.

Like the broken object is healed and proudly exposes its flaws, observe and accept your mistakes and your suffering. Cherish your scars! They show you the path you've already traveled. As proof of your experience and your past, they tell you: You have lived and survived! Don't linger on any memories that drag you down, but simply remember the progress you've made. You are reaching a new phase now.

Today, after all the ordeals I have lived through, I am ready for the next episode. In spite of it all, I still have confidence in the future. Or maybe, shall I say "thanks to" instead of "in spite of"?

Today, you are reaching a new phase too. Let go of what you need to let go of, and move forward! By evoking your suffering and the path behind you, contemplate your past to continue your progress without making the same mistakes again. Be mindful of your repetitive patterns and break the mold. Starting today, think and do things differently. Continuously conjugate your life from past tense to present and future perfect!

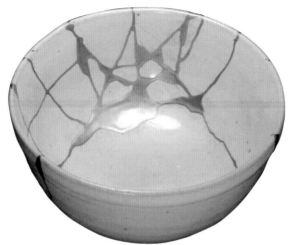

Kintsugi As Art Therapy

Today, several artists use the marvelous symbolism of kintsugi in order to complete a healing process.

The artists cover volunteers' scars with gold leaf during a gentle and at the same time strong ceremony to transcend them. By contemplating their exposed and magnified scars, the volunteers pick themselves up and find new inner confidence.

As a matter of fact, they often choose to leave the gold leaf on for several days after the performance so that it symbolically penetrates into themselves.

What About You?

Don't you feel deep inside that you are a survivor? This is the time to leave the past behind you and face the future with confidence.

It's Time to Act!

The Healing of the Past

Take another look at the graph of your life line prepared during the previous exercise. Does it remind you of something? This path, those difficulties, those broken lines . . . Don't they look like the scars of a broken object? Now is the time to transform these fault lines through a kintsugi process!

❶ Take a gold marker (available in all craft stores). You may also use a brush and gold paint.

❷ Close your eyes and reflect upon the special energy you would like this gold marker to carry: for instance, forgiveness, resilience, love, healing, joy, peace, or any combination of these.

❸ Mindfully and with much care, cover your life line with gold from your birth to today.

❹ Let it infuse . . .

Go Further . . .

If you wish, take another look at your now golden life line. As you would caress the scars of an object rebuilt by kintsugi, gently touch your fault lines with your fingers to measure the traveled path and to visualize the scars and healing of each phase. Proceed slowly and pause at any particularly painful "inflection" point.

Arrive at the end of the line, corresponding with your current age. Continue the line "virtually," going upward, visualizing all the good years full of gold and energy still ahead of you.

Start Here and Now!

Go and buy the gold pen or the golden paint!

A new force is with you!

FEEL

*The world breaks everyone
and afterward many are strong
at the broken places.*

—Ernest Hemingway

As the lacquer hardened while drying, feel how the object is even more solid than before.

Patiently, layer after layer, the kintsugi master has covered the cracks of the broken object with a thin film of lacquer. This natural balm from the resin of the lacquer tree progressively covered the scars of the object, fusing the broken pieces. Drying, it has prodigiously hardened. There is no turning back: They cannot be separated any longer; they have become one and the same.

It's thought that a kintsugi object is more solid afterward than before its metamorphosis. It is even said that some masters have the courage to test it and drop it for a second time!

My ordeals have also made me stronger. Now I feel that I have great inner strength. I survived, and I know I will be able to survive the next injury. It's almost like nothing can happen to me anymore. Or, better yet, like nothing can really hurt me. The cycle of life has its ups and downs, so it's impossible to be certain what the future might bring. But I have the impression that, no matter what happens, I have been reinforced, cured, and that I now know how to better manage the next challenges.

Just like kintsugi art, your flaws and weaknesses have reinforced you. What doesn't kill you makes you stronger . . . Now that you are consoled and consolidated, reinforced and hardened, nothing can impact you any longer: A new force is with you! Now, vigilant and experienced, you are the living proof that one can survive the toughest ordeals. You have been cured. You do, however, have to pay attention not to isolate yourself behind a thick shell: Leave yourself open to experience life.

The Force of Nature

Consolidation is a natural process: Just like kintsugi makes an object more resistant, so do many natural elements spontaneously fortify themselves after having suffered a shock or an ordeal.

Think of muscles that reconstruct themselves due to a protein synthesis around their fibers, bones strengthened after a break, burned earth that fertilizes itself from the ashes, hair and plants that grow more vigorously after having been cut, or burned wood that becomes harder and more resistant, and so on.

The Japanese have developed an entire art form around this last example, *shou-sugi-ban*, or art of burned wood. Boards are burned, scraped, irrigated with water, dried, and finally rubbed with finishing oil. Strengthened by a carbonized layer of wood, the core is now protected against ultraviolet radiation, moisture, temperature fluctuations, insects, and, ironically enough, fires! The finish has an intense and dark but brilliant beauty and over time develops a deep sheen.

Like nature, ordeals and challenges harden and reinforce us!

What About You?

Do you feel the strength of new forces circulating within you?

It's Time to Act!

Meditation of the Tree

To root this growing force within yourself, connect to the energy of a powerful tree. You can do so by simply closing your eyes and visualizing the tree. Certainly not a weak or frail tree, but a centenary tree in its full force, vigorous, stable, large, and well rooted.

Imagine, for example, a large centenary oak tree, a Lebanese cedar with expansive branches, a banyan tree with deep roots, or a baobab tree with a strong trunk expressing stability and strength.

Feel its energy. The sap circulating, its roots firmly digging into the soil, its rough trunk, its large branches, the wind that gently rustles its leaves. Minute by minute, its strength spreads into you.

You are becoming that tree. Incorporate it. Incarnate it. Become quiet, calm, and serene, just like the well-rooted tree. Breathe like it . . . deeply and gently, as long as you wish.

Then, slowly open your eyes again.

When returning to normal life, use that quiet strength whenever you feel the need.

Other images can also express this force: for instance mountains, elephants, or gorillas . . . Choose the energy that best suits you.

Go Further . . .

Next time you are walking in a park or forest, choose a tree that "speaks" to you and make a connection with its energy, sap, and roots. Adopt it. Some people even hug trees by embracing their trunks: That's the tree hug therapy. Follow your inspiration.

Start Here and Now!

To get started, put your hands on the next tree you come across and try to feel its energy.

Perfectly imperfect . . .

WELCOME

Well, nobody's perfect!
—From Billy Wilder's movie *Some Like It Hot*

Proudly accept the imperfections of the object. It is even more beautiful and precious once broken and repaired.

Here is the paradox of kintsugi: It is its very imperfection that makes it valuable. Its injuries make it priceless. Cured by gold, exposing its scars, it is that much more precious when the memories of the cracks remain visible.

The lesson to be learned from kintsugi is to understand the tyranny of perfection. Change your outlook, lift the mask, accept your flaws. Observe and embrace your weaknesses! They reveal that you are only human after all . . .

I first experienced this truth in a self-help seminar, where each person completely opened up to the group. At the end of the session, during a debriefing, we shared our feelings and indicated to the others how we perceived their essential selves and what had moved us. One of the participants said to me:

"Thank you . . . Your fragility is more beautiful than you will ever know! And furthermore, I believe that is where your own strength is rooted!"

Therefore, it may be time to see the value of your own path, your own "accidents," whether they are physical or psychological. They played a part in who you are. Today you have overcome them, and, paradoxically, it is thanks to them that you have developed your resilience and your new strength!

Sometimes the past reappears and tries to drag you down. Don't let it control your life any longer. Rather, proudly show your new self to the world, demonstrating what you are capable of. Straighten yourself with pride! Recognize the splendor, the force, and the beauty within you. They have always been there, but life's challenges have given you that little extra soul you needed to reveal them. Kintsugi teaches you to accept your authentic grandeur. Be proud of what you have become, of who you are . . . perfectly imperfect.

The Eulogy of Imperfection

Why is everybody striving for perfection? Would the *Venus de Milo* be as famous if she still had arms? Or the *Winged Victory of Samothrace* if she still had her head? On another note, which of Santa Claus's reindeer is the most famous if not the one with the red nose? And would the tarte tatin be as famous if it had been forced to stay in its mold?

In a world of mass production, often imperfections give value to objects by adding additional character.

For example, the Liberty Bell in Philadelphia, symbol of American independence, is an object of extraordinary affection in the United States. This enormous cracked bell is a true national icon. Its injury reminds U.S. citizens of the resilient force of the American democracy.

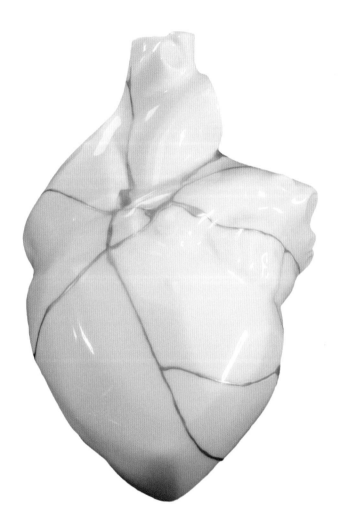

What About You?

Are you ready to let go of the tyranny of perfection and accept your fragility with pride?

It's Time to Act!

The Kintsugi of Your Rebirth

Whatever ordeals you have behind you, now is the time to officially recognize their cured scars by creating a kintsugi object that symbolizes your healing.

❶ Carefully choose an object that represents you or an injury you've suffered. For example, it could be an object in the shape of a heart, star, circle, dice, or diamond; a stone; or a painting . . . an object that makes sense to you. For instance, a person I know has chosen a mirror with a long family history. For myself, I have chosen a stone in the shape of a heart given to me by a very dear friend who found it in nature. She collects them whenever she takes a walk. It is one of her talents! She offered to let me choose one from her collection. I don't know why, because at the time I wasn't familiar with kintsugi, but I chose the only stone with a crack.

❷ If you do not own this particular object yet, obtain it. You can create it yourself out of clay, have a potter or glassblower make it to your wishes, or buy a finished piece such as a paperweight or a porcelain decoration. But first look around you. Could you perhaps own something already that might be suitable?

❸ If you like, you can also personalize it, using a method of your choice, like painting or engraving it with decorative elements such as initials or symbols embodying special feelings.

❹ Choose a fabric with special significance for you, and fold up the object in it with great care.

❺ This is the most difficult step. Grab a hammer and hit the object to break it, projecting into this action all the energy of your own injury and your own chagrin.

➏ Carefully gather all the pieces of the broken object.

➐ Mindfully follow the detailed instructions starting on page 11. Depending on your patience and means, you can choose the traditional method of repair or use a simpler, more modern approach.

➑ Contemplate your creation. It's official: You are now cured!

➒ Reflect and meditate on this thought . . .

Go Further . . .

Choose the best place to display it so you can contemplate it every day, as an invaluable daily reminder of your healing.

If you want, you can also share its story, your own story, on the website esprit-kintsugi.com to inspire other people and encourage them to take the resilience path you just initiated.

Start Here and Now!

Choose your symbolic object right now.

United with the universe

SHARE

Just as it is better to illuminate than merely to shine, so to pass on what one has contemplated is better than merely to contemplate.

—St. Thomas Aquinas

Present your creation. Share its history to inspire others that repair is possible.

The metaphor of kintsugi transmits hope and reminds us that things can actually be repaired. Proud of your progress, you now realize the beauty of your imperfect life path.

Why not let others benefit from your experience? Could the ordeals that you have overcome also be experienced by others? Today, cured after your initiatory path, you can inspire them with hope for their own resurrection.

For myself, I have long hesitated to reveal my personal flaws to others; the first version of this book was much more theoretical, without examples of my own life and the path I covered. Then a friend pointed out that in the phrase "personal development" is the word "personal," so I decided to throw myself, unprotected, into the water, and share all of my experiences. I thought this might make my writing more intelligible and maybe more inspiring too. Since I have been able to survive all of these challenges, coming out stronger than before, why not other people too? Why not you?

Yes, one can certainly survive this injury: You are living proof! You came, lived, and conquered . . . Now the moment may have come to transmit your own message and share what you've learned. Words can heal sufferings. By accepting your scars and admitting your flaws, you can encourage other people. No matter how you share it, your experience will give others confidence in their future. Maybe it's time to let the whole world know that you gathered all of your broken pieces and are now cured, reunited, ready for a new beginning. United with the universe.

© Myriam Greff

Art and Sublimation

The transcendence of suffering is a recurrent theme in the arts. Tortured by demons and traumas, artists often use their pains to transmute them. They play with the sensitivity of suffering and make it resonate at the center of their art. The spectators' feelings thus echo the artist's. In the same alchemistic process as kintsugi, the artist is transforming his lead into gold, transcending his pain into sublimation.

Examples of this abound. Think of the wrecked sculptures of César Baldaccini, the vibrations in the paintings by Van Gogh or *Guernica* by Picasso, the melancholy of the Romantic literature of the nineteenth century, or the most beautiful and sad love songs.

Let us leave the last word to Théophile Gautier:

Such in the Landes of our world is the poet's stance;

When he receives no wound, his treasure he'll retain.

With such deep cut mankind his heart must also lance,

To make him spill his verse, his gold tears' gushing rain!

What About You?

Are you ready to speak your mind and inspire hope?

It's Time to Act!

The Testimony of Your Renaissance

Depending on your skills and your focus, find you own mode of self-expression to inspire and pass on hope to others.

So would you prefer to:

- Have discussions with your friends about the subject?
- Participate in a conference to debate the sufferings you have experienced?
- Organize an exhibition of your challenges?
- Write a book about your healing?
- Organize a run to share energy with a group?
- Create a piece of art that expresses your suffering?
- Write a blog to share your experience?
- Participate in a television broadcast to talk about the subject?
- Create a club for people who have overcome similar traumas?
- Organize a fair to raise public awareness of a problem?
- Raise funding through charity events dedicated to this cause?
- Set up a stand-up comedy show about the subject?
- Produce a video or movie about your sufferings and how you overcame them?
- Write a song to sublimate your ordeals?
- And so on . . .

Go Further . . .

Inspire and motivate others so that they speak their minds too.

Start Here and Now!

Choose the media that appeals to you most, pick up the phone, write a first line, send the first e-mail, grab a paintbrush, take out your camera . . .

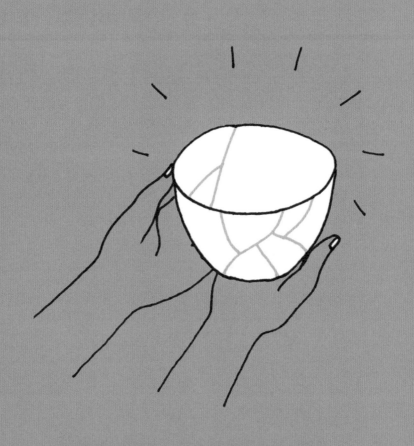

CONCLUSION

OPEN

人生は風前の灯火

jinsei wa fuuzen no tomoshibi

———————

Life is a candle before the wind.

—Japanese proverb

Don't demand that things happen as you wish, but wish that they happen as they do happen, and you will go on well.

—Epictetus

The art of kintsugi invites you to let go and to accept the impermanence of things. It teaches us to remain open to the unexpected, to imperfection, to serendipity, and coincidences . . . Japanese philosophy refers to this as *mushin no shin*, which means "thought without thought" (*mu*: "nothing/empty," *shin*: "heart/spirit"), calling to let things go.

As such, kintsugi is a great metaphor of our existence: The wheel turns, and life is unpredictable! Happiness and sadness, joy and sorrow, pleasure and stress, everything changes and evolves. Perfection and permanence are an illusionary trap. One can fight neither time nor change . . .

Now may be the time to detach . . . Could you have been able to predict all that has happened to you since you were born? Or at least during the last ten years or maybe even last year? Sometimes things turn out badly . . . and sometimes they turn out better than expected!

Could I have predicted, when I wrote my first tale at the age of six, that I had already found my true calling? When I was twelve, dreaming like all little girls, gazing at my mother's makeup, that I would realize my dream working for L'Oréal ten years later? When I was fifteen and addicted to fragrances, that I would be working with the greatest perfumers on the planet? When I turned twenty, attending a business school, that I would start my own company a few years later? When I was twenty-five and meeting my husband, that I would divorce him ten years later? When I turned twenty-six and got married, that I would be organizing and even celebrating other people's weddings? At thirty-five, after my divorce, having moved across the hall from my mother, that a year later I would be the one to discover her lifeless body? At thirty-nine, just when I had adjusted to my new life as a single mother, that I would marry one year later a high school friend I hadn't seen in twenty years?

When I turned forty, pregnant, getting married, happy again, that I would divorce one year later? And that at forty-one I would discover my real passion and true calling in the art of kintsugi that carried me to where I am today? So I don't fight it anymore; I let myself be surprised: Life, sometimes cruel and ironic, often gentle and well meaning, certainly has more imagination than I do. What new surprises does it hold for me?

Yes, life can turn things upside down in a day, minute, or second, one way or the other. Rather than burst through doors like a ram, I am encouraging you to let yourself be surprised: Sometimes a side door opens . . .

But I also invite you to remove your protective shield and armor. Do not put all of your treasures in a safe or at the bottom of a cabinet to protect them against inadvertent damage. On the contrary, savor and use them every day to give them a chance to be in touch with reality.

Maybe they will be broken by accident indeed. But only to become even more precious once covered and healed with gold . . .

Give life a chance to transform you: Take the Kintsugi-do, the Way of Kintsugi . . .

The Symbolism of the Cherry Blossom

Every spring, the Japanese celebrate *Hanami*, the cherry blossom (*sakura*) festival. This event is so popular that the weather channel even broadcasts the bloom forecast day by day!

These cherry trees are an ornamental variety and do not produce fruit. They exist only to be beautiful, without having any other function.

Full of elegance and rare splendor, they take your breath away. During a short two-week period, the trees lose their blossoms while blowing in the wind, shedding their delicate white and pink petals. This is an invitation to serene contemplation of life, its beauty, its short duration, and its fleeting happiness.

The wind that disperses each petal reminds us that nothing is permanent. Every moment, no matter how perfect, is only ephemeral. Enjoy it to the fullest . . .

© Myriam Greff

242

Playlist of the Kintsugi Spirit

To enhance your healing process with music, here is a very eclectic list of songs filled with the spirit of kintsugi. These range from grand classical pieces to classic rock, from Beethoven to the Beatles, with pop music, reggae, French songs, and hard rock. There is something for every taste! The only thing they have in common is their optimism and spirit of resilience.

- "Sandcastles" by Beyoncé

- "Gold" by Trinix

- "Feeling Good" by Nina Simone

- "What a Wonderful World" by Louis Armstrong

- "Wake Up" by AWOLNATION

- "Brand New Start" by Concrete Knives

- "Stronger" by Vandal

- "What Are You Waiting For?" by Nickelback

- "Here Comes the Sun" by The Beatles

- "Glorious" by Macklemore & Skylar Grey

- "Glitter & Gold" by Barns Courtney

- "I Will Survive" by Gloria Gaynor

- "Ain't Got No, I Got Life" by Nina Simone

- "Titanium" by David Guetta

- "Believer" by Imagine Dragons

- "Peace and Tranquility to Earth" by Roudoudou

- "Le Premier Jour du Reste de Ta Vie" by Etienne Daho

- "Golden" by Brandon Beal & Lukas Graham

- "Whatever It Takes" by Imagine Dragons

- "Let It Be" by The Beatles

- "Everything Works Out in the End" by Kodaline
- "1-800-273-8255" by Logic, Alessia Cara, Khalid
- "Harder, Better, Faster, Stronger" by Daft Punk
- "Beat It" by Michael Jackson
- "That's Life" by Frank Sinatra
- "Happy" by C2C & Derek Martin
- "Tubthumping" by Chumbawamba
- "Three Little Birds" by Bob Marley
- "C'est Ta Chance" by Jean-Jacques Goldman
- "Don't Worry Be Happy" by Bobby McFerrin
- "Bridge over Troubled Water" by Simon & Garfunkel
- "I Won't Back Down" by Tom Petty & the Heartbreakers
- "Happy" by Pharrell Williams
- "Anthem" by Leonard Cohen
- "Golden" by Jill Scott
- "Mon Everest" by Soprano & Marina Kaye
- "Avec le Temps" by Léo Ferré
- "Stronger (What Doesn't Kill You)" by Kelly Clarkson
- "Survivor" by Destiny's Child
- "The Show Must Go On" by Queen
- "Eye of the Tiger" by Survivor
- "I Believe I Can Fly" by R. Kelly
- "Fighter" by Christina Aguilera
- "Stronger" by Britney Spears

- "I'm Still Standing" by Elton John

- "Walk" by Foo Fighters

- "The Magic Flute" by Mozart

- "Alive" by Sia

- "Back in Black" by AC/DC

- "How Can You Mend a Broken Heart" by The Bee Gees

- "Spring" by Vivaldi

- "Believe" by Cher

- "Firework" by Katy Perry

- "Get Up, Stand Up" by Bob Marley

- "Träumerei" by Schumann

- "Wild Hearts Can't Be Broken" by Pink

- "Ode to Joy" by Beethoven

- "Gonna Fly Now" by Bill Conti

You can listen to this list at esprit-kintsugi.com and add your own suggestions!

Which songs would you like to add to this list?

GLOSSARY

Do: the way, the path, the route, the art of living mindfully leading to enlightenment.

E-urushi (or neri bengara-urushi): the second layer of lacquer used during the repair. Its color is red. The gold powder is added to it while the lacquer is still moist.

Gintsugi: seam covered with silver.

Kintsugi: seam covered with gold.

Kintsukuroi: mending with gold.

Mugi-urushi: glue to attach the broken pieces. It consists of a blend of resin (*urushi*) and flour. It is used when all the pieces of the broken object have been gathered.

Muro: cardboard box used as a container for drying.

Roiro-urushi: lacquer used to cover the cracks with a first layer after the initial repair. Its color is black.

Sabi-urushi: cement used to re-create and replace missing pieces, prepared from resin (*urushi*) and powdered stone (*tonoko*).

Tonoko: powdered stone blended with resin (*urushi*) to prepare the glue.

Urushi: natural resin from the lacquer tree, used in lacquer arts.

Urushi-tsugi: lacquered joint with a brownish-red color, before being covered by metal.

Wabi sabi: the art of living recognizing the beauty of imperfect, ephemeral, and simple things.

Yobi-tsugi: using a piece from another object to replace a missing piece.